TEACH YOURSELF BOOKS

CROQUET

INCLUDING GAMES FOR THE GARDEN AND THE CROQUET ASSOCIATION RULES

Don Gaunt

NTC Publishing Group

Long-renowned as *the* authoritative source for self-guided
learning – with more than 30 million copies sold worldwide –
the *Teach Yourself* series includes over 200 titles in the fields
of languages, crafts, hobbies, sports, and other leisure activities.

This edition was first published in 1993 by NTC Publishing Group,
4255 West Touhy Avenue, Lincolnwood (Chicago), Illinois 60646 –
1975 U.S.A. Originally published by Hodder and Stoughton Ltd.
Copyright 1992 by Don Gaunt

Printed in England by Clays Ltd, St Ives plc.

790
Gau

060789

——— CONTENTS ———

About the author

Don Gaunt first started playing croquet in the early 70s when he discovered a set in the basement at work. With some friends, he worked out the rules and started to play. Like many people, he had no idea that the game was played nationally and it wasn't until he moved to Ipswich in 1979 and joined the club there that he began to play seriously.

Since that time he has played in many events, both nationally and internationally. He was chairman of the Ipswich Croquet Club for several years before moving to Gloucestershire where he joined both the Cheltenham and the Bear of Rodborough Croquet Clubs. He was founder chairman of the Eastern Croquet Federation where he was instrumental in the creation of the Eastern Championships.

He has been a member of the Croquet Association Council for many years, with special responsibility for four of the season-long national tournaments. He is an examining referee and a qualified coach at all levels, being named 'Coach of the Year 1991'.

HOW TO USE
THIS BOOK

The purpose of this book is to enable you to teach yourself association croquet. Association croquet is the official version of the game in almost all countries of the world where croquet is played. It is also the version recognised by the World Croquet Federation for international events. *Note:* The term 'garden croquet' is often used, e.g. 'garden croquet set'. This is *not* a different version of croquet. It only refers to the place where croquet is played.

If you follow each chapter carefully you will, by the end of the book, be able to play croquet sufficiently well not only to enjoy the game but also to appreciate some of the subtleties of tactical play that croquet possesses.

Chapter 1 introduces the game with a brief history, followed by an outline of the rules. Read this chapter, perhaps using some counters on a piece of paper to help understand the moves. Do not try to play on the lawn yet.

Chapter 2 describes the equipment used. If you have not yet bought a set this may help you to choose. If you have a set already, it will tell you about the equipment in it. Thus armed, the last item to get right before playing is the lawn. The standard layout is shown, followed by suggestions on layout for those who have unusually shaped or small lawns.

In Chapter 3, play commences. You learn how to hold a mallet and how to strike a ball. A game is described which helps you to practise this.

Chapter 4 is perhaps the most important in the book. It describes in depth, the shot which is unique to the game of croquet – the *two-ball shot*. Read the chapter carefully, then practise the shots on a lawn.

Having learned the mechanics of the game, Chapter 5 shows how to actually play a game. It covers how to start, where to place balls, and tactics. Chapter 6 describes how to finish. Read these chapters first, then try out the ideas on a lawn.

The remaining chapters of the book cover topics which can be read separately. Chapter 7 describes ways of scoring. It also shows a method by which better players can be handicapped to make games more even. Read this chapter only when the basic game has been mastered. Chapter 8 contains a comprehensive reference list of the rules of association croquet. A number of games other than association croquet can be played on a croquet lawn. Chapter 9 describes how to play some of them.

For those who wish to proceed further with croquet, the final chapter gives information on joining the Croquet Association (the CA) or a club. It also gives a selected list of further books on the game.

Acknowledgements

No teaching book can ever be entirely the work of only one person. A good teacher is someone who passes on to others the knowledge gained from his or her own mentors. To this is added the teacher's personal experience. The result is, hopefully, a continually widening circle of knowledge. I hope that this book will widen the circle a little further.

My sincere thanks to those who taught me and to the following people who have made a specific contribution to the book. To Michael and Claire Hearfield for trying out the ideas. To Allan Parker of Parkstone Croquet Club and Tom Anderson of Wrest Park Croquet Club for contributions to the history chapter. To Peter Dorke of Ludlow Croquet Club for proof-reading the draft. To Martin French of Ipswich Croquet Club for comments on the rules.

I would also like to thank the following for their help with the photographs: Worthing Croquet Club for the cover, Tom Anderson for the Beddows Cup, Charles Townsend for the loan of a croquet set and Ipswich Croquet Club for the loan of their lawns.

1

— WHAT IS CROQUET? —

—— A brief history of croquet ——

The following description appeared in an account of an early croquet tournament held in 1872 at Wimbledon at the All England Croquet Club:

'Near the village of Wimbledon, on the very brink of the railway that hurries you thither and then bears off the rest of the passengers towards Southampton, Bombay, Jamaica, or wherever they wish to go, are four acres of grassy land. These acres are laid out in three terraces, the one above the other, and on each terrace are four croquet grounds. From a croquet point of view these grounds are simply perfection. Each is forty yards by thirty . . . beautifully levelled, and the yellows and pinks and blues of the rolling balls are resplendent in the sunshine.

Croquet in the eyes of experts is not a mania, nor the imbecility of first or second childhood. It is a very fascinating and very difficult game, requiring nerve, judgement, unremitting attention, and a great physical nicety . . . and I think we may almost say already that it is the most absorbing game yet invented . . . Early on Tuesday certain strange mallets, with their owners, were collected together at the Waterloo station – flat mallets, cylindrical mallets, heavy mallets, light mallets – and soon the Wimbledon croquet ground began to fill . . .'

It seems that the habit of making fun of croquet in articles existed even then, despite an obviously serious tournament played on good lawns with good equipment. It was not until 1877 that the first lawn tennis championship was held at Wimbledon, yet within five years croquet had virtually been ousted by tennis.

Despite this setback, croquet was flourishing:

> 'Croquet is a game of very modern invention, and yet, in a few years it forced its way into such extraordinary popularity, that there is not a parish in the kingdom where the game is not known – scarcely a lawn, suitable or unsuitable, where the hoops were not to be seen; scarcely a house of any pretensions above those of the labourer's cottage, in whose entrance hall or passage the long white deal box, which tells of mallets and balls within, was not a prominent object.'

So commences the Rev J G Wood MA, FLS, writing in *The Boy's Modern Playmate – A Book of Sports, Games and Pastimes*, published in 1893.

Yet Cassell's *Book of Sports and Pastimes Illustrated,* published only three years later, starts its section on croquet thus:

> 'Never, probably, has there been a game so universally and thoroughly popular in Great Britain as croquet, and never was a popularity so rapidly achieved or so soon undermined and thrown into the shade when its zenith had once been achieved'.

So croquet has had its ups and downs. The Edwardian era was probably croquet's highest point in terms of widespread play, while its lowest was to be during and just after the Second World War. It could well be argued, however, that in terms of availability to all, and in international recognition, croquet today is more widely played than ever before. One croquet equipment manufacturer estimates that there are now between a quarter and half a million people playing croquet in the UK.

The origins of croquet

How did croquet start? Many sources quote the game of Pall Mall as its origin. This was a game played in a straight line with large hoops and a mallet looking like a golf club. It had only a slight resemblance to modern croquet. It is not even certain that there is any connection between the game and the present Pall Mall in London. References give a variation of spellings such as Pallemaille and Pele Mele.

The name 'croquet' would seem to indicate a French origin, but it is quite likely that it was chosen simply for the sound. Cassell's *New French Dictionary* gives the definition of croquet as 'a game or a crisp biscuit'. It is interesting that the sticks which are used to indicate extra turns in handicap croquet are called bisques. The dictionary also gives one definition of crochet as a 'hooked stick' (shepherds crook?) and the verb croquer 'to crunch together'. Nothing is known for certain though, and the mystery remains.

The first known reference to a game that resembled proper croquet came from Ireland in the early part of the nineteenth century. The following is an extract from *Notes on Croquet and Some Ancient Bat and Ball Games Related to It* by R C A Prior MD, FLS in 1872:

> 'As to its introduction into this country the meagre result of all the enquiries that I have been able to make is only this: that I learned from Mr Spratt, of 18 Brook Street, Hanover Square, that more than twenty years ago a Miss Macnaghten brought it to him as a game that had been lately introduced into Ireland, but which she had first seen on the continent . . .

Around 1850, John Jaques, a toy manufacturer, produced a croquet set and his firm has been doing so ever since. There were, however, other manufacturers and many variations were to be found. Some of these were quite bizarre. For example, in one version a four-way hoop was set in the middle of the lawn with a bell suspended in the middle which had to be rung to finish. The number of hoops varied from six to ten, with one or two pegs. Even today there is a version with nine hoops and two pegs which is played in some places in America.

The developing game

As the century progressed, so did croquet. Clubs and associations began to be formed and the game spread round the British empire and even to America. As so often happens when a game becomes more popular, dissent started to occur and several rival organisations were created. Each of these claimed to be the true representative of the sport. Worse than this, croquet became associated with immoral behaviour. In England it was rumoured that young ladies would knock their ball into the shrubbery and would disappear with a young gentleman to look for it! In America things were even worse with, in 1890, the city of Boston banning the game.

By 1882, croquet had been ousted from Wimbledon by tennis and was in decline. Its revival commenced just before the end of the century. The United All England Croquet Association (later to become the present Croquet Association) was formed and by the outbreak of the Great War there were 170 registered clubs. These were the Edwardian days, considered by many to be the golden era of croquet. However, the war brought about the closure of many clubs, some of them for ever.

After the war, in 1918, croquet continued at a lower level. Two significant events to occur were the introduction of the advanced rules game for top players, and today's six-hoop and one peg setting.

The most radical change however was the 'either ball' rule. Previously, the balls were played in sequence. This meant that a player always knew exactly which ball was to be played next by his or her opponent. This ball would be put into a distant corner. It was then very difficult for the opponent to score. The new rule meant that at the start of a turn players could choose either of their own two balls to play with, irrespective of the one played on the previous turn. This rule, which is played today, makes the game much less one-sided.

The Beddows Cup

A problem which arose before and after the First World War was the loss of prestigious cups due to their being won outright. Nowadays cups can be won for one year only, but in the past, a cup won on three or four occasions was the winner's to keep. Some players re-donated them but others did not. One who did not was a Miss D D Steel. Tom Anderson from Wrest Park Croquet Club tells the story of the Beddows Cup.

'The Beddows Cup was the trophy for the Open Championships until 1933. That year Miss D D Steel from Bedford Croquet Club won it for the fourth time and was allowed to keep it. This trophy then disappeared from view in the croquet world.

I re-discovered the cup in 1978. Reading a local newspaper, I noticed an entry in the classified ads columns: "Bedfordshire Croquet Cup for Sale". The vendor, I discovered, was a local small antique dealer who was moving away and "wanted the cup to remain in Bedfordshire".

The cup is solid silver with large handles, about three feet tall, with a velvet lined box to hold it. It is very ornate, having a laurel wreath and crossed mallets surmounting the lid. There is a relief of a croquet scene all round one side of the cup, depicting a gentleman playing croquet and two lady spectators standing by a tent.

After seeing the cup we began to search for its identity. Looking through old Croquet Association records, we were able to correlate

The Beddows Cup

Detail from The Beddows Cup

the winners' names with those of the Beddows Cup. To avoid losing the cup again, possibly for ever, we purchased it, and have it to this day.'

The modern game

The Second World War saw an almost complete cessation of competitive croquet. It also resulted in the immediate or eventual closure of about half the clubs in the country. Picking itself up from this sorry state, the CA did what it could with what remained. By the 1950s, the major tournaments of the calendar were running well, and although there was not much growth, there was at least no deterioration.

The story from then to the present day has been one of a steady growth in popularity. Particularly satisfying has been the success of the CA in attracting sponsorship for major events, resulting in media attention which has helped to make the game more widely known.

Another success story has been the growth of new clubs. Thanks to efforts by the CA and regional croquet bodies, plus sterling work by bands of volunteers, several large and many small new clubs have been formed. Today it is rare for anyone not living in a remote rural area to be more than 30 miles from a club.

Recent years have also seen the emergence of expert young players. Although it is not true to say that they dominate totally, very many major events are now being won by teenagers.

Worldwide, croquet is co-ordinated by the World Croquet Federation. The rules of association croquet are the international rules used for the World Croquet Championships. These have been held since 1989. Croquet is widely played in Australia, New Zealand, South Africa, and the USA. It is also played to a lesser extent in Canada, France, Ireland, Italy, Japan, Spain, Sweden and Switzerland. Scotland, the Channel Islands, the Isle of Man and Wales have their own associations for administration, although they work closely with the English CA.

So croquet has come a long way in a relatively short time. Many things have changed, yet, again quoting from Cassell's book: 'It was the first successful attempt that had been made to invent an outdoor game in which both sexes could join on terms of equality, in which old and young could take part with equal chances . . .' These words are as true today as they were then.

──────── How to play croquet ────────

You may find it helpful to refer to fig. 1 throughout this section. *Note:* There is a glossary of terms at the end of the book.

The aim of the game

A croquet lawn is laid out with six hoops and one peg arranged as shown in fig. 1 on page 8. The object of the game is to get a ball through the hoops in the direction and order indicated. When a ball has passed through all hoops correctly, it can be made to strike the centre peg. It is then *pegged out* and has completed the game. The first player or pair to peg out both balls is the winner.

First principles

A game may be played by two people or four. Two play each other as 'singles', while four play in two opposing pairs as 'doubles'. There are four balls, each coloured differently. The usual four colours are blue, black, red and yellow. These colours will be used for describing play in this book. Sometimes you will see a set coloured brown, green, pink and white. These are called secondary colours and are often used when two games occupy the same lawn. Do not worry if your set has different colours. As long as you remember which player has which ball, the colour does not matter. Corresponding to the four balls are four coloured clips. These clips are placed on the top of the hoops to indicate which hoop each ball should pass through next. At the start of a game therefore, all clips will be placed on top of hoop one. As soon as a player successfully runs this hoop, he or she will move the correctly coloured clip to hoop two.

In singles, each player has two of the balls. It is conventional that the darker colours play the lighter. In this case therefore, blue/black plays red/yellow.

In doubles, each player has one ball and can only play with that ball during the match. However, there are not four individual opponents. The game is played with two pairs. Like doubles in tennis, the game is played as though each pair is a single unit, each individual in the pair playing his/her part as required.

The game starts with the toss of a coin. The winner/s can choose (a) to

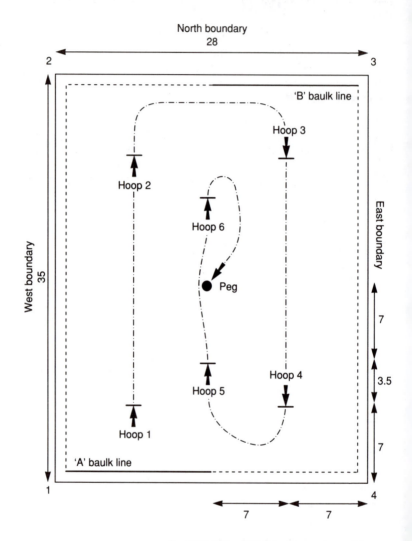

South boundary (All distances are in yards)

Fig. 1: The standard court

play first or second, or (b) what colours to play with. The loser/s therefore get whatever option is left. The winner will normally go for option (a) since there is usually no particular advantage in choosing colours.

A common misunderstanding should be corrected at this point. The peg will often have colours painted on it. This has *no* bearing whatsoever on the order of play.

Assume that the winner of the toss has chosen to go in first and that the loser has chosen red/yellow. Then either black or blue (in doubles, either the player of black or the player of blue) may play first. Assume black plays first. In the next turn the opponent(s) can play either red or yellow. Assume that it is red. Now blue must play next, followed by yellow. All four balls are now in play.

Having got all four balls into play, each side may opt to play the ball which is most advantageous. Thus blue/black may opt to play black for several turns in succession. (In doubles this would mean that one partner has several turns in succession.) Naturally no-one is allowed to strike a ball of the opposing side.

The starting point for each of the four balls is also shown in fig. 1. It is along one of the two lines marked 'A' baulk or 'B' baulk. Note that the baulk lines only extend half-way across the court. Fig. 2 shows the location of the line more clearly. The choice of baulk line and the position along it is made by the player. (It might appear logical at this stage always to choose baulk 'A', which is of course nearer to hoop one. However, later chapters show that the choice of baulk 'B' is often made for sound tactical reasons.)

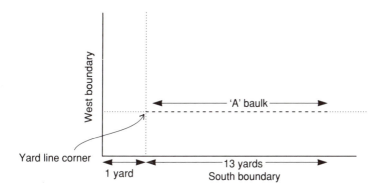

Fig. 2: The 'A' baulk line

Extra shots

The sections which follow, and others later in the book, describe various movements of mallets and balls. In order to avoid confusion it is important to distinguish between two quite separate movements: your mallet *striking* your ball, and a ball, while travelling across the court, *hitting* another. In this book therefore, strike, striking, etc. will mean your mallet striking your ball and hit, hitting, etc. will mean balls hitting each other.

If the only thing that could be done in croquet was to take it in turns to try to strike your ball through a series of hoops in sequence, the game would be trivial. Fortunately there are a number of ways in which your turn can be extended.

In snooker an extra shot is gained by potting a ball. Similarly, in croquet an extra shot is gained by striking your ball so that it passes through a hoop. This is called *running a hoop* or *scoring a hoop*. It has already been noted that each of your two balls (or in doubles, each partner's ball) must pass once through every hoop as shown in fig. 1. The diagram shows clearly that it might just be possible with a very accurate shot to run, say, hoop one, then with your extra shot, run hoop two. It would not be possible, however, to do the same between hoops two and three. More is therefore needed if progress is desired past hoop two within the same turn.

The game is extended still further by giving *two* extra shots if you are able to strike your ball so that it hits another. The way that these two extra shots are played is described below.

First extra shot

When your ball hits another, you pick up your ball and place it in contact with the ball that it has just hit. Then you strike your ball (not both) so that both balls move. The way that your ball is placed and the way that it is struck by your mallet determines how far and in what direction each ball will travel. Chapter 4 explains in detail how to do this.

Second extra shot

You then have one more shot with your ball only. With this shot you can either run a hoop or hit another ball.

Making a break

From the start (very first stroke) of your turn, you are allowed, if you wish, to hit each of the other three balls and place your ball next to it (as described above) once, without running a hoop. If you have hit all three and do not then run a hoop with your last extra shot, your turn must end. As soon as you run a hoop, however, you are once more allowed to hit all of the other balls. Irrespective of the way that this turn finishes, on your next turn, you can once again hit each of the other three balls.

So, with care and skill, it is possible to play so that the hitting of other balls, the subsequent striking of two balls placed together and the running of hoops, all combine to produce a situation in which many hoops can be run in a single turn. The tactics and skill required to make breaks in this way are what makes croquet such an interesting game. Croquet is not meant to be played in a negative fashion, concentrating solely on the destruction of your opponent. Played like that, it becomes boring. Played with prudent aggression and style, the game becomes an exciting challenge, with the rewards of a well-fought contest.

Finishing

A game is finished when both balls of a player or pair have run all of the hoops and then hit the peg. This may be done by hitting the peg with each ball in two separate turns. A better way, however, is to have your other ball (in doubles, your partner's ball) near the peg. Then, after the last hoop has been run, arrange your game so that you can hit your other ball. Your ball is picked up, and placed in contact with your other ball. With the first extra shot, cause your other ball to hit the peg. With the second, hit the peg with your own ball.

A pegged out ball is removed from the game, so if for some reason only one ball is pegged out, only the other ball can be played in subsequent turns (in doubles this means that only the player of the remaining ball can play). Chapter 6 describes in detail how to finish a game.

Other rules

Out of court

In the shot where you put your ball against the one you have just hit, neither ball must go out of court. If this happens the turn ends and any ball that went off is replaced on the yard line (see below). *Note:* In all other shots where a ball goes out of court, the ball is replaced on the yard line without any penalty.

There is an imaginary line one yard in from the boundary and parallel to it. It is on this line that balls are replaced if they go out of court. Fig. 1 shows the yard line. If a ball goes out of court within one yard of a corner, it is replaced on the yard line corner. Fig. 2 shows a yard line corner.

A ball passes out of court if any part of it touches or crosses the inside edge of the court boundary line. Fig. 3 shows this.

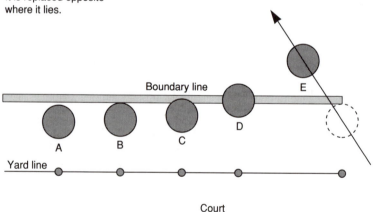

Balls B, C, D and E are out.
They are replaced at the point marked with a dot.
Note particularly ball E.
This was travelling at an angle,
and is replaced opposite the exact point where it went out.

Only ball A is still in court.
It is replaced opposite
where it lies.

Boundary line

E

D

A   B   C

Yard line

Court

Fig. 3: When a ball is out of court

Running a hoop

A ball has run a hoop, and scores a hoop point, when it passes through the correct hoop in the correct direction. The part of the hoop which faces the striker as he or she is about to run the hoop is called the *playing side*. A ball starts to run a hoop when its leading edge can be seen beyond the hoop on the non-playing side, when looking at the hoop side-on. A ball completes the running of a hoop when its trailing edge passes beyond the playing side and cannot be seen when looking at the hoop side-on. A ball may run a hoop in more than one turn, that is, having started to run in one turn, it can complete in another.

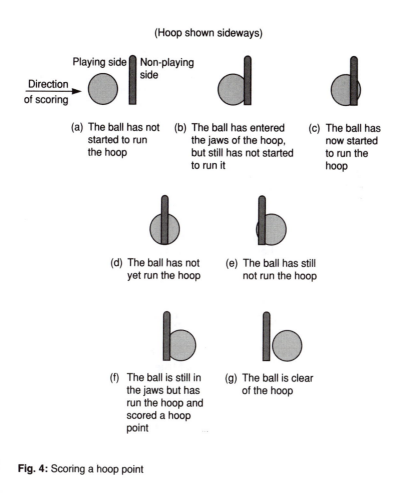

(Hoop shown sideways)

(a) The ball has not started to run the hoop

(b) The ball has entered the jaws of the hoop, but still has not started to run it

(c) The ball has now started to run the hoop

(d) The ball has not yet run the hoop

(e) The ball has still not run the hoop

(f) The ball is still in the jaws but has run the hoop and scored a hoop point

(g) The ball is clear of the hoop

Fig. 4: Scoring a hoop point

Fig. 4 on page 13 illustrates the scoring of a hoop point.

A ball other than your ball can be made to score its hoop; for example by sending it through its hoop when you hit it with your ball. This is called peeling. The clip for the peeled ball is moved to the next hoop for that ball.

Hitting the peg

Only a ball which has run all of its hoops can hit and score the peg or cause another ball to hit the peg. There is no penalty for hitting the peg with a ball which has not run all of its hoops.

Fig. 1 shows that six hoops are run in a single direction by each ball, plus one peg point for each ball, making a total of 14 points per player or pair of players. This is the most suitable version for garden croquet. However, it is possible to make a longer game by running the hoops again, but in the opposite direction. This longer game is described in Chapter 7.

Metrication

Croquet has not yet moved into metres and centimetres. To help those who do not use imperial measurements, a metric conversion of standard measurements is given in brackets. For example, the correct diameter of a ball is 3⅝ inches (92mm). In the case of many of the exercises, a measure has been used simply for convenience (for example, 'put the balls a yard apart'). In these exercises, for 'yard' read 'metre', 'foot' read '300mm', 'inch' read '25mm'.

Misunderstandings in croquet

One of the intentions of this book is to dispel the misunderstandings that surround croquet. The following are *not* true.

'Oh that's the game where you put your foot on the ball.' It is not, this is not allowed.

'It's a game played by old ladies.' Yes it is, but it is also played by women (and men) of all ages.

'Croquet is an elitist game.' No it is not, it is played by people from all walks of life.

'Ah yes, that's where you play with flamingoes for mallets.' If Lewis Carroll could have known the trouble he would cause, he would have never written that part!

'The idea of croquet is to send your opponent's ball into the shrubbery.' Not true, it is a fault to send a ball out of court.

'Croquet is a vicious sport.' This comes from the misconception that croquet is all about separating your opponent.

No doubt you will have heard others, plus all sorts of strange ideas on how to play. Well, there is only one set of rules in this country, and they are taught in this book – so please read on!

2

EQUIPMENT AND LAWNS

───────────── Equipment ─────────────

Mallets

It is possible to play with only one mallet, all sharing, but preferably each player should have his or her own. Shapes and sizes vary, but a typical mallet will have these characteristics:

- Weight about three pounds (1.4kg)
- Shaft length about one yard (0.9m)
- Head length about 9–12 inches (225–300mm).

For children, shafts may be shorter, but the weight should be the same.

Some mallets have round heads, some square. There is no advantage of one over the other, it is merely personal preference. Some mallets are even made of metal with plastic ends.

Care of mallets

Most garden set mallets are made entirely of wood. A regular coating of protective varnish will help preserve the mallet from damp. If the mallet gets wet, do not dry it too quickly. Store it in a cool dry place, either flat in a box, or hanging from a hook by the head. Do not leave it leaning against a wall as the handle may warp. If the mallet has a metal band at the ends, make sure that it does not protrude and damage the balls (or people).

Balls

These may be of compound, plastic or, occasionally, wood. They should weigh about one pound (454g) and have a diameter of 3⅝ inches (92mm).

Care of balls

If the balls are of wood, the same care should be taken as for mallets except that paint of the appropriate colour is used instead of varnish. No special care need be taken with compound or plastic balls as far as normal use is concerned.

Underweight mallets and balls

If your croquet set is of very light construction, an enjoyable game of croquet can still be had, but some care needs to be taken. Very hard shots on heavy lawns should be avoided as there is a danger of breaking the mallet shaft.

Some croquet strokes (see Chapter 4) may not be possible with an underweight croquet set. In particular:

• With light mallets (less than 2lbs) roll strokes will be difficult.
• With light balls (less than ¾lb) stop shots will be difficult.
• With light balls *and* light mallets, croquet strokes in general may not behave exactly as predicted in this book.

Clips

Where provided these should be used as described in this book. If they are not provided, wooden clothes pegs painted the appropriate colours will work well.

Flags and corner pegs

These are not essential to a game, but if your set has them, fig. 35 on page 105 shows where they should be placed.

Hoops and peg

The best hoops are those of sturdy metal construction, using five-eighths of an inch diameter uprights and a welded square top. These are, however, expensive and less robust hoops may have to suffice. If your hoops are of the thin wire variety, they will work well for normal play but very hard shots where the ball hits the hoop should be avoided as damage can result.

If you have a hoop with a blue painted top, make this the first hoop. If you have a hoop with a red painted top, make this the last hoop. Any other colours can be ignored.

Setting the hoops

Unless the ground is soft, it is better to make pilot holes first with a spike. Use a wooden mallet to drive the hoops and the peg into the ground. If you do not have one, place an old piece of wood on top of the hoop and strike that. Make slight adjustments to the width of a hoop by packing the sides of the holes with grass cuttings or earth. The width of the hoops should be a quarter of an inch (6 mm) wider than the balls. Check that all the balls are the same diameter. If they are not, use the widest ball for setting the hoops.

Croquet sets

Many sports shops sell croquet sets, although you will probably need to go to a larger shop to obtain the better quality sets. Often, the national associations for each country (see Appendix 1) will sell croquet equipment. The first photograph in the colour plate section shows a middle-of-the-range croquet set. Such a set will sell for around £175. Simpler sets are available at around £100. If you want a complete set of championship standard equipment, it could cost you around £1000.

Appendix 2 on page 129 provides a list of manufacturers of croquet equipment around the world.

Lawns

The ideal lawn is perfectly flat, closely cut and a symmetrical rectangle with the dimensions shown in fig. 1. Only a lucky few with big gardens can hope to approach the ideal, but good play is still possible on small, and even oddly-shaped lawns.

These simple guidelines will improve playing conditions considerably:

- Cut the grass reasonably short. Bowling green standard is normally not possible but playing on grass an inch long is difficult and unpredict-

able. Do not cut your lawn *too* short if it is bumpy or on a big slope. If
you do so, it will be very difficult to control the direction of the balls.

- Clear the lawn of any huge weeds, especially near hoops. Large
  weeds will often deflect a ball.
- If possible, move hoops occasionally to even out wear on the grass.

Small and odd-shaped lawns

The regulation dimensions of 35 by 28 yards (32 by 25.6 metres)
represent a large lawn. This is about the size of two tennis courts, but a
perfectly satisfactory game can be had on a much smaller area. Even a
piece of ground 10 by 5 yards (9 by 4.5 metres) will do, although there
are obviously very few really difficult shots on something that small.
Anything smaller than this is not really practical for six hoops. If this is all
that is available, set out three hoops in a triangle with the peg in the
middle, and run them twice, going through in the opposite direction the
second time.

The measurements given in fig. 1 should be reduced in the same ratio as
the lawn. So half length or width equals half the measurement.

Irrespective of the size of the lawn, keep the yard line at one yard. This is
so that play within the yard line area can take place normally. However, if
you only have the tiny lawn with three hoops mentioned above, you could
reduce the yard line to half a yard.

Strange-shaped lawns can make for some very interesting games! Fig. 5
on page 20 gives a few suggestions for some common shapes. Note that
in each case the order and direction of hoops is kept similar to the
standard layout.

If you have a tree or other obstruction in the lawn, make a local rule that
there is a free movement of balls if your swing is impeded by the tree.
However, such movement must not give an advantage. For example,
you should not have a clear shot at a ball if none existed from the original
position. Also, any ball hitting the tree and bouncing off is played where it
lies (subject to the swing rule just given).

If you have a small flower bed or similar in the middle of the lawn, treat
this as a boundary in the same way as the normal boundary, i.e. your turn
ends if you go over the edge.

So, you now have a lawn and a croquet set plus a general idea of the
game. It's time to start striking a ball.

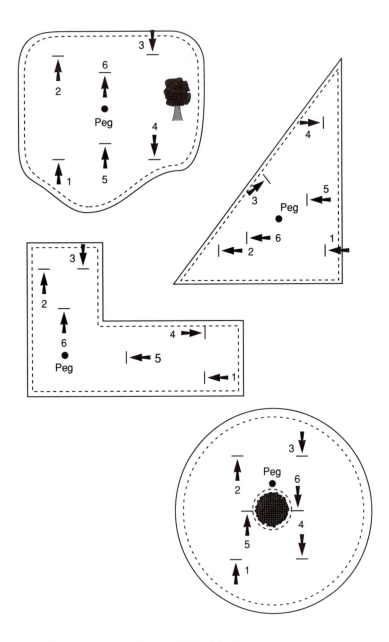

Fig. 5: Some non-rectangular lawns laid out for play

3

– STRIKING THE BALL –

——— Holding your mallet ———

Stance

There are two main ways to stand when taking a shot. These are called the centre and the side styles.

In the centre style, which is the most common, you face the ball directly and in line with the direction in which you intend to send the ball, standing with each foot equally spaced either side of the ball. You then swing the mallet between your legs.

In the side style, you still face the direction in which you intend to send the ball, but stand to one side of the ball. You either keep your feet together, or place one slightly in front of the other – whichever feels most comfortable. Your mallet is swung parallel to the side of your body. Normally, right-handed players would play to the right and left-handed players to the left but the mallet may be swung from either side – the choice is personal.

There are other, less common styles. The mallet can be held and played like a golf putter or a cricket bat. A few players find this suits them but it is unusual.

Celia Steward demonstrates the side style in photograph 2 in the colour section, while photographs 3–5 all show centre style, but with different grips (see page 22). Notice in each picture how the player is facing along the line of strike.

Grip

There is no 'perfect' way of holding a mallet. The important thing is to find a grip which suits you. This section describes the most common types of grip. It is recommended that you experiment with them to find the most suitable.

The standard grip

Photograph 2 in the colour section shows the so-called standard grip. It *is* a very common grip, but there is no such thing as a standard way of holding a mallet. Celia has her left hand at the top of the mallet and her right hand about a foot down the shaft. Notice that she is holding her left thumb over the top of the shaft, and her right index finger is pointing down the shaft. It is not essential to do this, but many players who use the standard grip do so because they feel that it helps them swing the mallet more accurately. You should hold the mallet in a way that feels comfortable for you.

In photograph 3, the author, who is a left-handed player, is also using a standard grip, but his hands are held much closer together. He uses the index finger for guidance, but not the thumb. Having the hands closer together helps the arms swing as a single unit, but makes the mallet more difficult to control.

The Irish grip

1991 World Champion John Walters is using the Irish grip in photograph 4. This grip is good for balancing the arms and is extremely accurate when played well. It does, however, take a lot of getting used to, and places a lot of strain on the wrists. If you find that you like this style, do not play too much croquet at first, or your wrists will complain!

The Solomon grip

Named after John Solomon, a champion player, the Solomon grip is demonstrated by Celia Pearce in photograph 5. As you can see from Celia's arms, this is a very symmetrical grip. It is frequently used by players who adopt method two of striking the ball (see page 26). Like the Irish grip, the Solomon needs practice and can be hard on the wrists.

Other grips

Many players adopt grips which are combinations of the above. Try the exercises below, and find out which suits you best.

EXERCISES

1 Experiment with centre and side stances and see which feels the best for you. Hit a ball to get the feel of the stance but don't worry about what happens to the ball, concentrate only on the stance.

2 Experiment with the different grips and see which feels the best for you. Hit a ball to get the feel of the grip but don't worry about what happens to the ball, concentrate only on the grip. Be aware that those grips which have the hands close together will often need a longer time to get used to than those with the hands further apart. Don't fix on a grip for all time at this stage, but do give the one that you choose time to work.

– Striking the ball to hit another ball –

Although the ability to send a ball in the required direction is only part of croquet, it is a vitally important part. If you do not hit another ball or run a hoop, you will not get any more shots and your turn ends.

To hit another ball, imagine a piece of string joining the centre of your ball with the centre of the one you want to hit. Now extend that string beyond the balls. Stand well back from your ball, facing both, and walk slowly towards your ball along the imaginary string. Stop about a foot from your ball and take stance (centre or side). The correct positions are shown on page 24. If you look ahead, you should be looking directly at the other ball. If you look down you should be looking straight at your ball. Your mallet should be resting lightly on the ground, directly facing the ball in the direction in which you want to send it.

This procedure is called *stalking the ball.* Its purpose is to ensure that your body is correctly placed so you are facing in the same direction as the line formed by the imaginary string.

The exact distance to stand behind the ball will come with practice. If you are tending to strike your ball with the bottom of your mallet, you may be too far back. If your ball jumps in the air when you strike it, you may be too close (sometimes this happens if you lean forward just as you go to strike your ball).

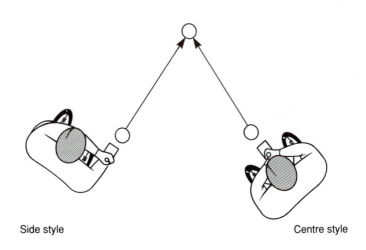

Side style   Centre style

Fig. 6: Taking your stance

Playing the shot (1)

Having taken the correct stance, line up your shot. This can best be done by taking a few practice swings over the top of the ball. Then rest your mallet on the ground, directly behind your ball and compose yourself for the shot.

The actual shot can be split into three parts: the backswing, striking the ball and the follow-through.

The backswing

It is during the backswing that you are lining up your mallet to strike your ball. Your backswing should therefore be sufficient to allow you to do this. If you only take a very short backswing, you are likely to jerk the mallet off line. There is no 'correct' amount of backswing but your mallet head should travel about a yard before hitting the ball for a fairly firm shot. This travel can be reduced for shots that are less forceful but there should always be some swing. In photograph 6 in the colour section, the author is attempting to strike his ball onto the peg. Notice the amount of backswing used, and his concentration on the ball.

The strike

Don't force the mallet to change direction at the end of the backswing. Let it change naturally. The secret of a good swing is to 'let the mallet do the work'. If you find that hitting the ball is an effort, you are not letting the mallet work for you. If you swing sweetly, you will strike the ball sweetly. In photograph 7, the ball has just been struck. Note that the centre of the mallet head has struck the ball.

The follow-through

Just as the backswing is important in getting the mallet on the right line, so the follow-through is important in keeping it there. Your mallet should be allowed to stop moving naturally – do not force it to do so.

Photograph 8 shows the ball striking the peg, but the striker is not looking at the ball. This is because his follow-through is only just finishing. Note the position of the mallet and the striker's head.

An essential ingredient of any good shot is to keep your eye on the ball during the backswing and strike. In fact it is fairly easy to watch the ball at this stage, but it is the most natural thing in the world to follow the mallet head up after the strike to see where your ball is going. The most natural, and totally wrong! Keep your eyes on the spot where the ball was until the follow-through is complete. By doing this, you will keep your mallet on the right line. Photographs 6–8 illustrate this point.

Throughout the three parts of the shot there is a common thread – keep it smooth. Watch any player of any sport where a ball is struck. The best shots seem to be played without effort. The same applies to croquet.

Some other hints

Do . . .

- Practise your swing before striking your ball.

- Make sure that you are facing the ball. Your practice swings should help. Imagine that you have struck your ball and follow the line of your swing, to see where the ball would go.

- Stand firmly but not stiffly.

- Move the whole of your arms as a single unit. Swing from the shoulders, not the wrists.

- Keep an even, firm but not tense grip with both hands.

Don't . . .

- Stand stiffly upright with your arms held rigidly down, making a sort of lunge at the ball. This is a common and understandable fault with beginners because there is a lot to remember.

- Move or lean forward before your follow-through is over. A symptom of this happening is that your ball jumps in the air when you hit it. Be careful though, as long clumps of grass can give the same effect.

- Twist your wrists.

- Grip more firmly with one hand than the other.

- 'Bounce' as you swing through. This is caused by excessive bending of the knees as you swing.

Playing the shot (2)

This is an alternative method of playing the shot. It is one adopted by many of the top young players. It is extremely accurate when played properly, but many find it more difficult to execute than the method described above.

Having stalked the ball and taken the correct stance, line up your shot by taking practice swings over the top of the ball. When you have the line correct, drop your mallet on the final backswing and strike the ball. The secret is to play the final swing which actually strikes the ball in exactly the same way as the practice swings.

The comments made in the previous section regarding backswing, the strike and follow-through apply equally to this method of play. So also does the remark about a smooth shot.

Keeping your eyes on the ball is also as vital, but more difficult because you do not have that period when the mallet is static behind the ball in which to compose yourself.

EXERCISES

For each exercise, try both methods of playing the shot to see which suits you best.

1   From one yard away, make your ball hit another.

2   From five yards away, make your ball hit another.

You can consider yourself successful if you can regularly:

- For 1: hit the ball nine times out of ten.
- For 2: hit the ball five times out of ten.

—— Striking the ball to run a hoop ——

Much of what has been said about hitting another ball applies when attempting to run a hoop. There are, however, a couple of extra points to consider.

Even when directly in front of a hoop, you must be very accurate with your shot, since the gap is only a little wider than your ball. When you are at an angle that gap becomes very small indeed. So lining up and stalking the ball are vital. When directly in front of a hoop, you naturally aim for the centre of the gap. When you are making an attempt from an angle, your aiming point moves towards one of the hoop uprights. If your shot is from the right of the hoop, the aiming point moves to the left and vice-versa. Fig. 7 illustrates this. As shots become more angled, the aiming point will move further across. Eventually, you will find yourself aiming directly at an upright. You have then reached the limit beyond which it is not possible to run the hoop.

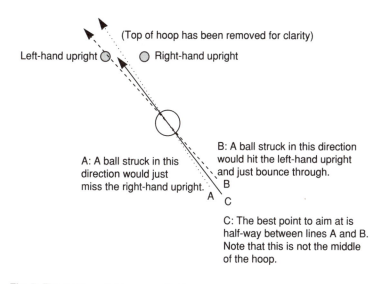

(Top of hoop has been removed for clarity)

Left-hand upright ○   ○ Right-hand upright

A: A ball struck in this direction would just miss the right-hand upright.

B: A ball struck in this direction would hit the left-hand upright and just bounce through.

C: The best point to aim at is half-way between lines A and B. Note that this is not the middle of the hoop.

Fig. 7: The aiming point for an angled hoop

The comments previously made about keeping your eye on the ball hold here as well. The temptation to look up immediately to see if you have successfully run the hoop is great. Resist it, you will know soon enough!

Photograph 9 in the colour section illustrates the technique of hoop running.

EXERCISES

For each exercise, try both methods of playing the shot to see which suits you best.

1   From one foot away and directly in front, make your ball run the hoop.

2   From one foot away and six inches to the side, make your ball run the hoop.

You can consider yourself successful if you can regularly:

- For 1: run the hoop nine times out of ten.
- For 2: run the hoop seven times out of ten.

Strength of shot

You have now seen how to strike your ball, either to hit another or to run a hoop. This section considers how hard you should play the shot.

Against another ball

You will recall from the description given in Chapter 1 that if you hit another ball with your own, you lift your ball and place it in contact with the ball you have hit. You can then play a shot which sends both balls in the required direction.

The ball that your ball hit in the first instance will have moved to a new position. Exactly where that new position is will be determined by the strength and angle with which your ball has hit it.

For example, suppose that you want to run a particular hoop. Your ball is directly behind (a few inches) the other ball, in line for your hoop, which is three yards away. If you only hit the other ball gently, the two-ball shot which follows (you will recall from Chapter 1 that you have two strokes, so you will be using one to get in front of the hoop and the other to run it) will take place nearly three yards from the hoop. If, however, you hit the other ball so that it travels the three yards to the hoop, your two shots take place right next to the hoop.

If the ball that you are going to hit with yours is very close to your own, it should be possible not only to hit it in a straight line but also (if needed) off-centre, so that it travels at an angle. Very close means no more than a couple of feet away.

Through a hoop

There will often be a ball waiting at the other side of your hoop. This ball will be used to continue your break when you have run the hoop. Chapter 4 shows how to put that ball there, in readiness, before you run the hoop. The strength with which you run the hoop will depend on the position of that ball.

If you are running the hoop from an angle, you will need to use more force than you would for a straight shot at the same distance because some of the energy is lost as the ball hits the hoop and bounces off. Care is needed, though, because the harder you strike a shot, the less accurate you tend to become.

Take particular care when your ball is very close to the hoop. It is not a fault to hit the hoop with your ball, nor is it a fault if you simply strike the hoop with your mallet. However, it *is* a fault and your turn ends if you 'crush' your ball against the hoop with your mallet. A crush occurs when the mallet strikes the ball in the direction of the hoop or peg without any room for follow-through. This is avoided by striking the ball away from the obstruction, allowing for free movement. Although a crush seems difficult to judge, it is usually fairly obvious to you as the striker. You are honour bound to admit the fault, replace the balls to where they were before the fault, and end your turn.

One useful tactic when your ball is close to the hoop is to give the ball a little flick with your mallet. Your mallet will then stop quickly and will not crush your ball.

EXERCISES

1 From one foot away, strike your ball so that it hits another, causing it to move for three yards in a straight line.

2 From one foot away, run a hoop and pass through by one yard.

3 From one foot away, run a hoop and pass through by three yards.

You can consider yourself successful if you can regularly:

- For 1: get the ball within two feet of where you want it.
- For 2: get the ball within one foot of where you want it.
- For 3: get the ball within one yard of where you want it.

Golf croquet

Despite its name this game is neither golf nor croquet! It is a simple game which is ideally suited to learning the skills which are described in this chapter, since nothing further is required other than a few simple tactics. It can be played with two players having two balls, four players with a ball each, or four players as two pairs. A turn is one single strike of your ball – there are no extra strokes in golf croquet. With that stroke you can do one of three things (occasionally you can do two of them in the same shot):

- Run a hoop (see law 3).

- Hit another ball.

- Take position, for example to run a hoop next time.

Balls are played in rotation (see law 8). If four people are playing, this means that each person has one shot in turn. If two are playing then players alternate both turns and balls, i.e. player A plays blue, player B plays red, player A plays black, player B plays yellow, etc.

The aim of the game

A game starts by spinning a coin. The winner chooses to go first or second, or colours, in the same way as association croquet. Each ball must be played into the game from anywhere on the 'B' baulk only. As soon as one ball has run a hoop, all players move on to contest the next one. A ball has to completely run a hoop in one turn. If it sticks, it has to come back (*Note:* this is *not* the same rule as association croquet). The exception to this rule is if your ball is knocked there by an opponent (not a partner). In this case you can run next turn (if it is still there). Each hoop scores one point. The winner is the one with the most points after all hoops have been run.

Rules of golf croquet

1   The contest is for six hoops, starting with hoop one and finishing with hoop six in the order shown in fig. 1 on page 8.

2   Each player has only one shot per turn. Play is strictly in sequence (see law 8). The shot may be used to (a) take position, (b) knock another ball out of the way or (c) run a hoop.

3   A ball runs a hoop in the same way as in association croquet (shown in fig. 4 on page 13). Unlike association croquet, if a ball starts to run a hoop but does not complete the running, i.e. it sticks in the jaws, it cannot score in the next stroke and must come back to try again. *Exception:* if the ball is placed there by an opponent it can run the hoop next turn.

4   When a ball runs a hoop, one point is scored for that ball's side and everyone moves on to the next hoop. *Note:* only *one* ball scores the hoop, not all.

5   There are six hoops, thus six points. When a player or side reaches an unbeatable score, i.e. scores four points, the game finishes and that player is the winner. If the score is three points each after the sixth hoop, continue (from where the balls lie) back to hoop one as a decider.

6   The game starts from anywhere along the 'B' baulk.

7   Any ball which goes out of court or into the yard line area is replaced one yard inside the boundary line from the point where it went off.

8   The normal sequence of play is blue, red, black, yellow. For second colour sets, the order is green, pink, brown, white. For other coloured sets, decide before playing.

9   The peg plays no part in the game except as an obstruction.

10   The game described is a short version. For a longer version see Chapter 7.

11   If two hoops are run in the same stroke, the striker scores two points and the game moves on two hoops.

12   Players must all contest the same hoop. A player is not allowed to assume that a hoop will be scored and so place his or her ball in advance for the next hoop.

13 If a player plays out of sequence, all balls are replaced and the correct player plays.

14 If a player plays a wrong ball, all balls are replaced and the correct ball is played.

Basic tactics

- Remember that golf croquet is a sequence game. Thus if you are playing red and cannot run the hoop, then black is the danger ball as black plays next (see law 8). The blue ball is less of a threat, but remember that black could hit yellow out of the way and yellow is the ball which precedes blue.

- When you are hitting balls out of the way, you may be able to do so in a way which puts your ball in front of the hoop.

- Instead of hitting an opponent ball, you can sometimes prevent a shot by putting your ball in the opponent's way.

- You can sometimes hit your partner ball and knock it in front of the hoop.

- If you are behind a hoop, you can block an opponent by jamming your ball in the hoop. Remember that you must clear the hoop in order to run it yourself.

4

— TWO-BALL SHOTS —

- The importance of the two-ball shot -

In Chapter 1, a two-ball shot was described as follows: *When your ball hits another, you pick up your ball and place it in contact with the ball that it has just hit. Then you strike your ball (not both) so that both balls move. The way that your ball is placed and the way that it is struck by your mallet determines how far and in what direction each ball will travel.*

Before the two-ball shot is explained more fully, it may be helpful to introduce a few croquet terms which describe this sequence. The hitting of another ball with your own is called a *roquet*, and the movement of the ball that you have hit is called a *rush*. The first extra shot – striking the two balls when placed together – is called the *croquet stroke* or *taking croquet* and the second extra shot is called the *continuation stroke*. Because these terms will be used a lot in this chapter, they are listed below so that you can refer to them easily. A full list of terms is included at the end of the book.

Roquet   – hitting another ball with your own.

The roqueted ball   – the ball that you have just hit. *Note:* when you play the croquet stroke, this ball becomes the croqueted ball.

Rush   – the movement of the roqueted ball when your ball hits it.

Croquet stroke   – striking your ball when it has been placed in
(also **taking croquet**)   contact with the roqueted ball.

The croqueted ball   – the other ball (not your ball) in a croquet stroke. *Note:* before taking croquet, this ball was called the roqueted ball.

Continuation stroke   – the extra shot that you have with your ball
after a croquet stroke.

Although many sports require the accurate striking of the player's ball,
and, in some cases, the subsequent hitting of others, it is only croquet
that requires the accurate movement of *two* balls in a single stroke (in
snooker it is a foul shot to move a ball that is touched by the cue ball).

The croquet stroke not only sets croquet apart from other stationary ball
sports, it can truly be said to be central to the game. To strike one ball
through a hoop requires skill, but to move two balls at the same time *and*
position them with accuracy is much more challenging. A croquet player
who can hit accurately will be quite successful, as will one with a good
grasp of tactics. The player who can also play good croquet strokes will
be formidable indeed. The croquet stroke is so important, this chapter is
devoted almost completely to it.

It has to be said that croquet shots are easier to describe than to do.
While there are a few lucky 'naturals' at the game, most of us mortals
have to try very hard to make croquet shots work. So do not be surprised
or disillusioned if things seem to go badly at first. Keep at it! It takes time
but suddenly it will all click into place and you will start to play well.

First, a look at what leads to a croquet shot – the roquet.

Roquets and rushes

To be able to take croquet, you must make a roquet – i.e. hit another ball
(see page 23). Note, though, that you take croquet from where you have
rushed the roqueted ball (i.e., when it has stopped moving), not from
where you originally hit it. Fig. 8 shows this.

This means that the rush is important in itself, not just something that
happens as a result of making a roquet. With skill and planning you may be
able to rush a ball to a part of the lawn where it will be much more useful
than in its present position. The next chapter shows some of these useful
positions.

EXERCISES

1   With your ball one foot away from another, roquet and rush the other ball
for three yards in a straight line.

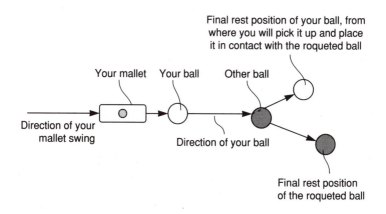

Fig. 8: Making a roquet

2 With your ball one foot away from another, roquet and rush the other ball for ten yards in a straight line.

3 With your ball one foot away from another, roquet and rush the other ball for one yard at an angle like that in fig. 8.

You will have grasped the idea if you can regularly:

- For 1: get the rushed ball within two feet of where you want it.
- For 2: get the rushed ball within three yards of where you want it.
- For 3: get the rushed ball within one foot of where you want it.

The croquet stroke

Definition

A croquet stroke is played by first placing your ball in contact with the roqueted ball, then striking your ball so that both move. Fig. 9 illustrates a typical croquet stroke.

You can see from fig. 9 over the page that the two balls move off in different directions. Why? Well, it all depends on the direction in which you strike your ball. Suppose that the croqueted ball had not been there in fig. 9. Your ball would naturally have travelled in the same direction that you struck it. The croqueted ball *is* there, however, so that some of

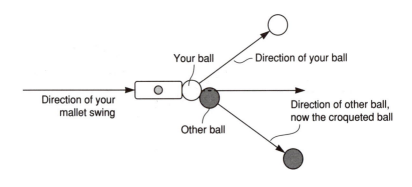

Fig. 9: A croquet stroke

the energy put into striking your ball passes through to the other one (this is why they have to be in contact – if they are not the shot does not work properly).

Prediction

Can you then predict where the balls will go? Yes you can.

The croqueted ball will travel along a line drawn through the centre of both balls. It will also travel at an angle from the line of your mallet swing. Your ball will travel at the same angle in the other direction. In other words, if the croqueted ball moves away at 20 degrees to the left, then your ball will move away at 20 degrees to the right.

'Very interesting', you say, 'but what does it mean?'

If fig. 9 is redrawn as fig. 10 and some lines are added, things will be clearer.

The movement of the croqueted ball is the easiest to predict. It is *always* going to travel along line A in fig. 10. So imagine this line on the lawn, then place your ball behind the other and on that line. Fig. 11 (opposite) shows how to choose two different directions.

To predict the direction of *your* ball requires more care. Look at fig. 10. The croqueted ball travels along line A. Your ball travels along line C. Your mallet swings along line B. So you are aiming at half the angle

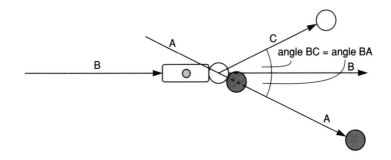

Fig. 10: A croquet stroke showing angles

To send the croqueted ball towards X, place your ball here

Note that as long as the croqueted ball *does* move, it will go towards X or Y irrespective of the direction in which your mallet swings

To send the croqueted ball towards Y, place your ball here

Fig. 11: Lining up the croqueted ball

between lines A and C. If you want to get technical the angle between lines A and C is twice that between lines A and B or between lines B and C.

But there is an easier way!

Execution

By repeating fig. 10 as fig. 12 and this time putting in another line (D) which joins the two balls after they have moved, you can see that line B (the one you swing your mallet along) crosses line D exactly halfway between the two balls. So you don't have to worry about angles unless you want to. Just look at where you want the two balls to go and *aim half way between them*. You can see this clearly in photograph 10 in the colour section. Celia wishes to place red in front of her hoop (on her left), and yellow behind it. In photograph 11, she has achieved this. If you compare the ball positions in 11 with the position of Celia in 10, you will see that she plays her croquet stroke by aiming midway between where she wants the two balls to go, i.e. just to her right of the hoop. Notice in 11 how Celia is carefully lining up the hoop stroke before taking her stance.

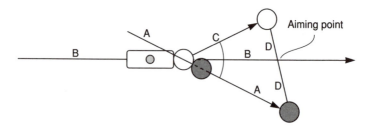

Fig. 12: The aiming point for your mallet

A summary of how to play a croquet stroke

(a) Decide where you want the croqueted ball to go, then draw an imaginary line back to where it is at the moment.

(b) Put your ball on this line, behind the other ball and touching it. The imaginary line should now pass through the centre of both balls (like line A in fig. 12).

(c) Decide where you want your ball to go.

(d) Aim halfway along a line (line D in fig. 12) joining the final positions of both balls.

(e) Strike your ball.

EXERCISES

1 Place two balls and your mallet in the same position as in fig. 12. Place two coins a few yards away on the two imaginary lines A and C. Judge the correct aiming point and strike your ball. Watch to see if the balls travel over the coins.

2 Repeat the exercise above for different angles.

You will have grasped the idea if you can regularly get the ball to cross within one foot of the coins.

Note: Do not make the angle too wide. Also, apart from noting where the balls come to rest so that you can judge line D, do not worry about the relative distances each ball travels. This is covered next.

Strength

Now you know how to get the balls to move in the correct directions. The next thing to master is getting them to travel the correct distances. To see why this is necessary, place two balls in contact for a croquet shot and then make the following experiments:

1 Strike your ball so that both move in the same direction. Note that your ball only goes about a quarter of the distance of the other.

2 Now strike at the angle shown in fig. 9. This time both balls travel approximately the same distance.

3 Finally, strike your ball at almost right angles to the other. The croqueted ball hardly moves while yours goes a long way.

The previous section of this chapter described how to calculate and play angled shots. In these experiments, the angle at which your ball moves in relation to the other varies from nothing, where both balls go in the same direction (experiment 1), through an angle (experiment 2) to almost 90 degrees – i.e. at right angles (experiment 3). It is *almost* 90 degrees, because at right angles or more, only your ball will move and the rules say that both balls must move. From this you can see that the nearer your angle is to 90 degrees the greater will be the movement of your ball in relation to the other.

So, although the relative distance that each ball will travel can be altered, to achieve this you have to alter the angle of shot as well. This is not a very satisfactory situation. You need to be able to control the relative distance that each ball travels independently of the angle. The way to do this is similar to snooker: you put varying amounts of spin on your ball when you strike it.

No spin

This is known as a *drive shot*. It is the normal shot described in Chapter 3 'Striking the Ball'. It should also have been the shot you used for the three previous experiments. No spin is put on your ball with this shot but that does not mean that it is no good. In fact there are many situations where it is exactly the right shot. Also, it is easier to play than the shots that do impart spin.

EXERCISES

1   Place two balls in contact and try some drive shots, sending both balls in a straight line, and observe what happens to each ball.

2   Try some drive shots at various angles and observe what happens to each ball.

Top spin

This is known as a *roll shot*. It puts top spin on your ball, making it go further than it otherwise would have done. To play a roll shot, slide your hands down the mallet shaft into the position demonstrated by Jill Waters in photograph 12 in the colour section. As mentioned in Chapter 3, putting your index finger down the mallet shaft is a matter of personal choice. Note that her finger does not actually touch the mallet head, because it would be a fault to do so. Now strike your ball and follow through in the manner illustrated in fig. 13, and photographs 13–14.

In photograph 13, Jill has taken stance and is ready to play the shot. Although a centre-style player, Jill plays roll shots from the side. This is because she, like many players, finds a centre-style roll shot too awkward. Note the position of her hands, feet and mallet, and also that her eyes are firmly fixed on her ball. To play the shot, Jill swings back, keeping her arms, hands and mallet together as a single unit, and her body still. Shen then swings forward, passing through the same position shown in photograph 13. As with other shots, follow-through is most important. Photograph 14 shows this. It also shows both balls travelling off together.

The amount of 'roll' that you obtain depends on a number of things.

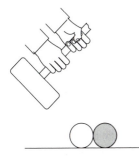

(a) Just before striking your ball

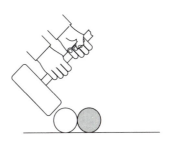

(b) At the point of striking your ball

Note: The position of the hands are shown for illustration only. For a more accurate view of hand positions, see the photographs which demonstrate the roll shot.

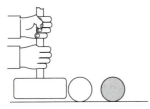

(c) Half-way through the shot

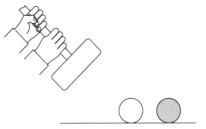

(d) The follow-through

Fig. 13: The roll shot

These are the two most important:

1   How far up your ball you hit it. Up to a certain point, the closer your mallet strikes to the top of the ball, the more the roll – i.e. the further your ball goes relative to the other. Beyond that point your ball digs into the ground and the shot is ineffective. Fig. 14 illustrates the range over which a roll shot works properly.

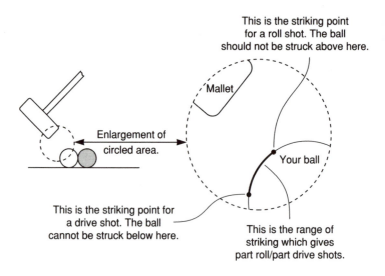

Fig. 14: The effective range for a roll shot

2   How far down the shaft you hold the mallet. This is not precise but generally, the lower down you hold it, the more roll you can get. Remember that you are not allowed to touch or hold the mallet head.

The roll shot is not an easy one to master. To help you, here are some useful hints.

● Keep your eye on your ball. This has already been stressed in the last chapter, but it is very difficult to remember when you are so close to your ball and you are concentrating on getting all of the other things right as well. If you find yourself missing the ball or catching the top of it, you are probably moving your eye.

● Swing through smoothly. If you jerk at it the balls will squirt off in odd directions. If you stab into the ground, nothing much will happen!

- Swing through quickly. There can be a tendency to slow the swing down because you are so close to the balls. If you do this you will maintain contact with your ball for too long and push it in the direction of your mallet instead of it going off at the angle intended. As well as the shot going wrong it is also a fault to push your ball (this is true in all shots although it is most likely in the roll).

- Swing through in the right direction. Yet again, the closeness produces a tendency to swing in the direction you want your ball to go instead of the 'half-angle' point described earlier. You are probably making this fault if you find that your ball goes too wide in angled roll shots.

EXERCISES

1 Place two balls in contact and play a roll shot in a straight line so as to get both balls to travel five yards.

2 Try the same shot for ten yards.

3 Try some roll shots at various angles and observe what happens to each ball.

You will have grasped the idea if you can regularly:

- For 1: get both balls within one yard of where you want them.
- For 2: get both balls within three yards of where you want them.

Back spin

This is known as the *stop shot*. It has the opposite effect to a roll shot, i.e. your ball only travels a short distance compared to the croqueted ball. Snooker players can get back spin by striking under the cue ball. This is not possible in croquet as the mallet face is too big. Some small amount of spin can be achieved by dropping the mallet swiftly down to the ground at the exact point when your mallet strikes your ball.

Fig. 15 and photographs 15 and 16 illustrate the stop shot. Note in photograph 15 that although Celia is holding her mallet in the same way as for a drive or single-ball shot, the front of her mallet is raised very slightly. In photograph 16, Celia has just struck her ball. Note that her ball has moved only slightly, while the croqueted ball has moved a long way. Her mallet rests on the ground at the point of impact.

The amount of 'stop' that you get depends on two things:

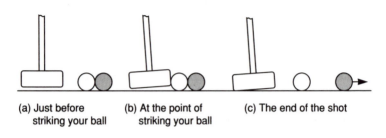

(a) Just before
    striking your ball

(b) At the point of
    striking your ball

(c) The end of the shot

Fig. 15: The stop shot

1   How quickly you stop the mallet after the mallet has struck your ball.
    The grounding of the mallet to give back spin helps achieve this but
    some people play stop shots by simply stopping the mallet in mid-
    swing just after it has struck the ball. In comparison tests that the
    author has carried out with a colleague there seems to be little
    difference in the results for either method. Choose therefore the
    method which you find easiest to play and gives the best results.

2   How quickly you drop your mallet. The quicker it is done the more
    the spin. However this is not a very important part of a stop shot so
    don't try too hard at it.

The stop shot may take some practice to master. To help you, here are
some useful hints.

● Keep your eye on your ball. This is as true here as it is for the roll. If
  you don't, you will find your mallet stopping short of the ball.

● Keep the action smooth. The stop shot is of necessity one with a
  sudden finish but that does not mean it should be jerky. If you jerk at it
  the 'stop' action will not be as effective.

● It can often help with this shot if you move your feet a few inches back
  from your normal stance. Doing this helps you to lift the front face of
  your mallet as shown in fig. 15 and photograph 15.

EXERCISES

1   Place two balls in contact and play a stop shot in a straight line so as to
    make the croqueted ball travel ten feet while your ball travels one foot.

2 Try the same shot, making the distances ten yards and one yard.

You will have grasped the idea if you can regularly:

- For 1: get both balls within one yard of where you want them.
- For 2: get both balls within three yards of where you want them.

Side spin

Although a tiny amount of side spin can be put on your ball, it lasts for a very short time and has virtually no effect. For practical purposes side spin can be ignored.

A summary of the croquet stroke

Playing the complete croquet stroke can be summarised as follows:

D I R E C T I O N	(a) Decide where you want the croqueted ball to go, then draw an imaginary line back to where it is at the moment. (b) Put your ball on this line, behind the other ball and touching it. The imaginary line should now pass through the centre of both balls (like line A in fig. 12). (c) Decide where you want your ball to go. (d) Aim halfway along a line (line D in fig. 12) joining the final positions of both balls.
S T R E N G T H	(e) Note the distance that each ball has to travel. (f) Remember that the wider the angle the more your ball will travel relative to the other. (g) Decide how much 'roll' or 'stop' is needed. (h) Play the stroke.

The table opposite gives pointers to the type of shot to play by saying what happens in different situations.

Note: In Chapter 2, mention was made of the different characteristics of balls and mallets which were not of standard weight. If your set is like this, you will not get exactly the same results as those shown opposite. Play all of the shots and take careful note of any differences. Also see what type of stroke is needed so that the balls *do* move as described in the table.

EXERCISES

1 Play all of the shots in the table of distances on page 47. Do not worry too much about the strength of shot but check that the relative distances are as described in the table.

2 Play the shots again but this time choose appropriate distances for each ball, then try to play a shot with the correct strength to achieve your objective.

You will have grasped the idea if you can regularly:

● For 1: get both balls to do what the table says.
● For 2: get each ball to go where you want it plus or minus 30%.

Combination shots

As you start to improve at croquet strokes, try to combine some of them. By doing this you can get the two balls to move to exactly where you want them, instead of just somewhere nearby.

For example, suppose the angle you require is zero and that you want your ball to travel half the distance of the croqueted ball. The table opposite shows that when the angle is zero, a drive does not send your ball far enough if you get the croqueted ball right, while a roll sends it too far. You can combine a roll and a drive by sliding your hand only part way down the mallet shaft and by striking your ball half-way between the drive and the roll points (fig. 14). This shot is called a *half roll*. Other combinations give quarter roll, three-quarters roll, etc. If you look at photograph 13, Celia is playing a partial roll shot.

EXERCISES

1 Play the shot in photograph 13, varying the amount of roll until the shot produces the correct result shown in photograph 14.

Angle of shot (between balls)	What happens when you play:		
	A normal drive	A roll	A stop
Angle = 0 The balls are played in a straight line.	Your ball travels between a third and a quarter of the distance of the croqueted ball.	Both balls travel about the same distance.	Your ball travels about a tenth of the distance of the croqueted ball.
Angle = 10° The balls split apart a little.	Your ball travels about half the distance of the croqueted ball.	Your ball travels a bit further than the croqueted ball.	Your ball travels about an eighth of the distance of the croqueted ball.
Angle = 45° The balls split apart quite a lot.	Both balls travel about the same distance.	Your ball travels a lot further than the croqueted ball.	Your ball travels about half the distance of the croqueted ball.
Angle = 85° The balls split apart widely.	Your ball travels a long way while the croqueted ball hardly moves at all.	There is no point in playing a roll as a drive is better.	The stop has virtually no effect on your ball so play a drive shot.

Table of relative distances

2   Try a half roll sending the balls at an angle.

3   Choose three random points on the lawn. Take croquet from one of them and try to send the balls to the other two. See if you can find out what is possible and what is not.

Take-off shots

If you look at the table on page 47, you can see that when the angle is large, the rules described so far break down. In fact what happens is that your ball no longer splits off at an angle but goes in the direction in which you strike it. It behaves almost as if there were no croqueted ball there. This is actually rather useful! It means that if you want to leave the croqueted ball where it is you can do so and just concentrate on your ball.

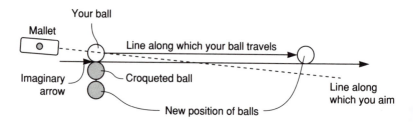

Fig. 16: The take-off shot

This type of shot is called the *take-off* because your ball takes off from the other one, leaving it more or less where it was (but remember that for it to be a legal shot, the croqueted ball must move – even if it is only a fraction of an inch).

To play a take-off shot, refer to fig. 16. The balls are placed in contact (this is still a croquet stroke), so that the imaginary arrowhead points in the direction that you want your ball to go. Then, strike your ball in the direction shown, imagining that you are striking just a single ball.

EXERCISES

1   Play a take-off shot, sending your ball ten yards while not moving the croqueted ball more than one foot.

2 From one corner spot, take-off to within five yards of another corner.

You will have grasped the idea if you can regularly:

- For 1: achieve the shot stated.
- For 2: achieve the shot stated without sending the croqueted ball off the court.

The continuation stroke

Having successfully played the croquet stroke, you now have one more stroke, the *continuation stroke*. This is used to do one of four things. The four options are given below in the order in which they are most likely to be chosen.

(a) To roquet another ball

You will then play a croquet shot.

However, you can only roquet a ball that you have not roqueted before. If you have already roqueted each of the other three balls without making a hoop, you cannot make any more roquets this turn. You must choose between options (b), (c), or (d).

(b) To run a hoop

Running a hoop not only gives you an extra shot, but also you are now allowed to make a roquet on each and any of the other three balls.

You will then play option (a), (b) or (c), but not (d), depending on the situation having run the hoop.

(c) To take position somewhere

You would do this if options (a) or (b) were not possible. Since your turn is going to end after this shot, the most likely place will be somewhere near your partner ball. This move is discussed in more detail in the next chapter.

You then have no more shots.

(d) To scatter another ball

This is the least likely shot to take. Nevertheless it is useful to note that even if you are not allowed to roquet another ball it is still permissible to knock it out of the way in much the same way as you can in golf croquet. The balls then remain where they lie (or are replaced if they go off court).

You then have no more shots.

EXERCISES

1 From various positions around a hoop, including behind it, do the following:

(i) Choose a direction in which to run the hoop.

(ii) Place two balls on your chosen spot, ready to take croquet. It is recommended that initially you do not play from closer than six inches or further than three yards from the hoop.

(iii) Play a croquet stroke so as to put your ball in front of the hoop ready to run it. The croqueted ball should be sent to the opposite side of the hoop and about two yards beyond it. An example is shown in fig. 17.

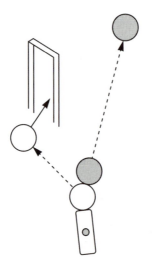

Fig. 17: Exercise 1

(iv) In your continuation shot, run the hoop.

(v) Having run the hoop, roquet the other ball again.

2 From various positions around the lawn, do the following:

(i) Place one ball (x) somewhere on the lawn.

(ii) Choose a spot from which to take croquet.

(iii) Place two balls on your chosen spot, ready to take croquet.

(iv) Decide where to send the croqueted ball.

(v) Play a croquet stroke so as to put your ball to within a yard of the previously placed ball (x). The croqueted ball should be sent to within a yard of its chosen spot. An example is shown in fig. 18.

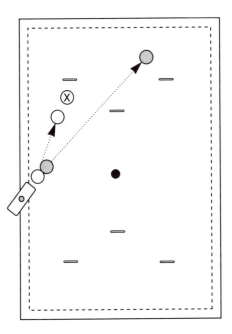

Fig. 18: Exercise 2

(v) In your continuation shot, roquet ball x.

You now know all of the basic strokes. It is time to start a game.

5

—— MAKING A BREAK ——

The first four chapters have given you an introduction to the game, how to choose and set out the equipment, the way to play shots, and detailed instruction on control of the balls. It is now time to consider an actual game. There are many ways to start a game but the one described here is used more than any other.

—————— Starting a game ——————

Fig. 19 shows the positions of the four balls when they have been put into play as described below.

The first ball on the lawn

You have chosen to start from the 'A' baulk. However, it is not a good idea to go straight for the first hoop. If you bounce off it you will leave an easy target for ball two. If you do make the hoop, what do you do next? You cannot safely shoot for hoop two as you will be close to the 'B' baulk if you miss. So you have to go somewhere safe. It is not worth the risk for just one hoop. The correct place to put ball one is near corner four. This makes a long shot for ball two. Even if hit, making hoop one from there is difficult.

The second ball on the lawn

Assume that ball one has been placed near corner four. For the reason described above, it is not very productive to shoot at ball one. Ball two should be placed to *'lay a tice'*. A tice, short for entice, is one which

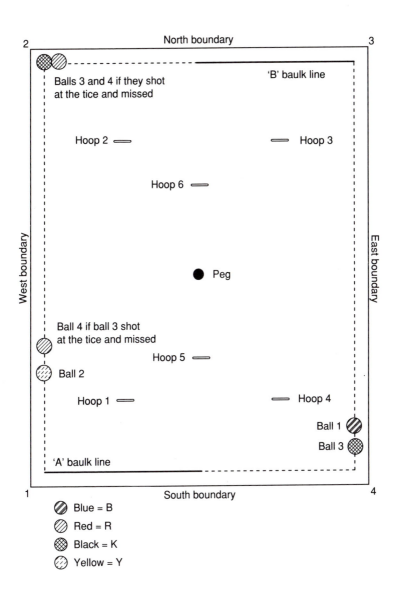

Fig. 19: Positions of the balls after the start of a game

tempts your opponent to shoot at it, but is sufficiently far away that he or she misses. Some cunning is needed here because you have to be a judge of what your opponent thinks is a tempting tice! A typical place to send your ball is along the west boundary about eight yards down from corner one. Shoot at this point from half-way along the 'A' baulk.

The third ball on the lawn

The player of ball three has two main choices now:

(a) Shoot at the tice from corner one

If this is hit, with your croquet stroke send ball two to about three-quarters of the way towards hoop two from hoop one. Then with your continuation stroke, 'join up' with ball one, i.e. put your ball close to it.

If, when you hit the tice, you happened to rush it to the correct position, play a take-off to ball one and roquet it with your continuation stroke. Then, in your next croquet stroke, roll both balls to a position about seven yards from corner four, down the east boundary. Finally, with your last continuation stroke, give yourself a foot-long rush to hoop one.

If you miss, you should have struck your ball sufficiently hard that it ends up in or near corner two.

(b) Join up with ball one

Shoot from the centre court end of 'A' baulk to put your ball off court so that it is replaced on the yard line about a yard away from ball one. By doing this you are putting the pressure on your opponent to hit his or her own tice (see below). Do not actually shoot at ball one: the chances of hitting are small and if you miss you could well leave a *double target*. A double target is two balls so close together they increase greatly the chance of the opponent hitting.

The fourth ball on the lawn

By now there are many combinations of things that can have happened. The two most common are:

(a) Ball three has shot at the tice and missed

Shoot at ball two from half-way along the 'A' baulk. If you miss, you are joined up. If you hit, roll to a *'guarded leave'* for hoop one. Guarded leaves are explained later in this chapter.

(b) Ball three has joined up with ball one

In this situation you cannot join up because doing so will leave two balls near hoop one which could be used by your opponent to make that hoop. So, as stated above, there is some pressure to hit the tice.

Shoot at your tice from corner one with sufficient strength to go to corner two if you miss. The reason for striking hard is that you do not want to have two balls close together near hoop one when your opponent is already joined up.

If you hit, play a take-off shot to balls one and three. Roquet one of them, then play a take-off shot to a position behind the other so that you have a rush to hoop one. With your continuation stroke roquet and rush to hoop one. (If this all seems a bit complicated, don't worry, the sequence is described in detail in the next section.)

In other words, by hitting the tice you have given yourself a chance of running hoop one and maybe hoop two and maybe . . . You are in fact starting a break.

—— The definition of a break ——

A definition of a break was given in Chapter 1:

With care and skill, it is possible to play so that the making of roquets, the subsequent croquet strokes, and the running of hoops all combine to produce a situation in which many hoops can be run in a single turn.

A turn where more than one stroke is played (and, hopefully, one or more hoops are scored) is called a break. It should be a player's objective at the start of a turn to make a break, because:

- by making a break, more hoops are likely to be scored.

- running several hoops in one turn gives your opponent less opportunity to score than running each hoop individually.

- scoring hoops in a break is often easier than scoring them individually.

- making a break is a very satisfying and rewarding thing to do. It also makes for a good game of croquet.

———— How to make a break ————

In this next section, and some others which follow, some time will be spent describing the movement of balls around a lawn. To make it easier to follow the diagrams, the following conventions have been used.

1 It is assumed that one player will be using red or yellow. This player will be called ROY. The other player will be using blue or black and will be called BOB.

2 To make things easier to see, hoops and balls are drawn much larger than they should be with regard to the scale of the lawn.

3 A key identifies the coloured balls on each diagram.

4 The initial and subsequent positions of balls are marked in curly brackets. The initial position on the diagram is always 1. So the initial position for red is shown as {R1}, etc. Black is shown as K {K1} to distinguish it from blue {B1}. Only significant movements are recorded on the diagrams to avoid cluttering them, so {R3} is the third significant position of red and not necessarily the third actual position in play. To help you understand what is happening, where there is a text description to go with a diagram, the significant positions are cross-referenced into the text.

The section above, 'Starting a game', finished with the player of ball four shooting at the tice. Assume that ROY is playing red and has hit this tice (yellow) {Y1}. This is shown opposite in fig. 20. BOB is close together near corner four {B1}{K1}. Yellow was originally in position {Y1} but was rushed to position {Y2} when red hit it. ROY takes off to BOB's balls near corner four. Because this shot is a take-off, yellow only moves a little, so this is not shown in the diagram. Red is struck from position {R1} (in contact with yellow) to position {R2}. From here he has an easy shot to roquet black. Black is rushed off court by this. It is replaced on the yard line {K2} and red prepares to take croquet from black.

A brief word on replacing balls on the yard line. Since the yard line is not marked on the lawn, it is a good idea to measure your mallet and note or mark on it a point which is one yard long. This will make replacement of the ball easier. Note that it is the centre of the ball which is placed on the yard line, not the inside edge.

Fig. 21 over the page gives the new position of the balls. Red plays a short take-off shot into the yard line area so as to obtain a perfect rush

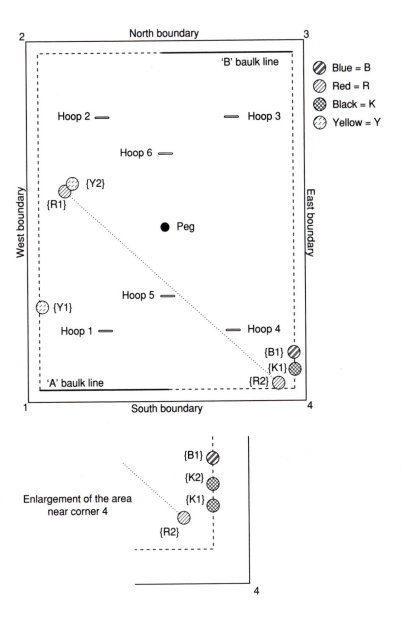

Fig. 20: Making a break after hitting the tice (a)

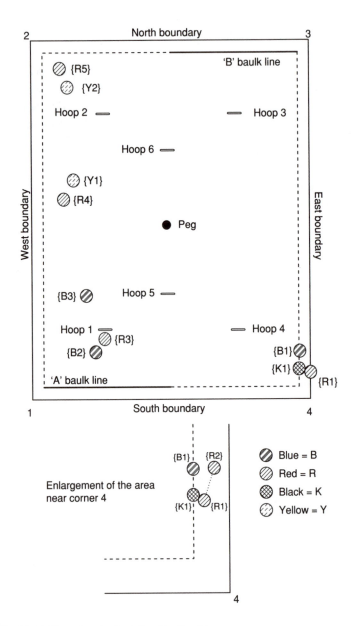

Fig. 21: Making a break after hitting the tice (b)

towards hoop one, position {R2}. Note that red is *not* replaced on the yard line. The rule is explained in the boxed section.

The yard line rule

The yard line area is that part of the court which is between the yard line and the edge of the court, i.e. it is a one-yard strip round the inside edge of the court. Any ball which goes into the yard line area is replaced on the yard line at its nearest point to the ball when it has stopped moving (see fig. 3).

This rule does *not* apply to your ball when it is entitled to a continuation stroke. It is entitled to a continuation stroke after a croquet stroke and after running a hoop. In both of these cases if your ball goes into the yard line area it is played from where it lies.

So if you play a croquet stroke which sends both balls into the yard line area, the croqueted ball is replaced on the yard line but yours is not. (Note that if either ball goes off court, rather than in the yard line area, your turn ends. See Chapter 1, 'other rules'.)

So with your continuation shot you have a rush to hoop one {B2}. This is similar to the exercise on page 50 in Chapter 4, on roquets and rushes. If you achieve this, your objective will be to send blue beyond hoop one to position {B3}, while putting red in front of hoop one, position {R3}. This is similar to the exercise on page 51 in Chapter 4.

Red will now run hoop one. Blue has conveniently been placed on the far side of the hoop and is waiting to be roqueted (remember that having run a hoop, you can roquet all of the balls again). Red can then take-off for yellow near hoop two {R4}. With skill and luck, you will get a rush to hoop two and run it. If you do not, you can use the last croquet and continuation shots to set up a rush for red towards hoop two using yellow {R5}{Y2}.

So, the result of this turn has been the running of hoop one and possibly of hoop two. Not only that, you have separated blue and black and you have left an opponent's ball near yellow's hoop while having a rush to the red's next hoop. Not a bad start! You have made a break and retained control of the game.

EXERCISE

Set up balls in the positions shown in fig. 20, just after the tice has been hit. Follow the book and try to run hoops one and two. In this, and all exercises in this chapter, try to get each shot exactly as shown in the book. If it does not work, replace the balls for that shot and try again. Make three attempts at getting it right. If you still have not succeeded, place the balls in their correct positions and carry on, noting that this particular shot is one you should practise.

Problem 1

How might the above break be modified so that hoop three could be run in the same break? Play your solution and see if it works.

In this and other problems, it will help if you draw a diagram. If your solution is different to the one given in the book, try both – you could well come up with a better one! All problems assume a full-size lawn. If you have a smaller lawn, modify any distances given in the problems accordingly. Answers to this and all problems at the end of the chapter.

How to use the rush to create breaks

The rush is very useful when trying to make a break because if you have a good rush, you can send the roqueted ball where you want it. There have been a couple of examples of this already. In the first, where the tice was hit, red obtained a rush on blue that put blue in front of hoop one instead of near corner four. The second example formed part of the solution to Problem 1.

Another useful thing that you can do with a rush is to get behind a boundary ball, as in fig. 22 opposite. Suppose red is part-way along the east boundary, on the yard line and near hoop four {R1}. You have just run hoop two {B1}. You hoped to get a rush on yellow {Y1} (the ball you used to approach hoop two) towards hoop three. Unfortunately you did not, but you did get a rush towards red. A hard rush sends yellow off court near red. Yellow is replaced on the yard line {Y2} (remember, it is not a fault to rush the roqueted ball off court). A little take-off shot will now give you the required rush towards hoop three {B2,B3}.

The rush can also be used to give yourself easier croquet shots – see the next section under 'drive shots'.

So whenever you play a croquet stroke with the intention of moving your ball to a position where it can make a further roquet, look to see if a rush will help. If you already have a rush lined up, make sure that you know how hard you want it to be. Finally, if chance gives you a rush, don't just take it because it is there! Check first to see if you need one.

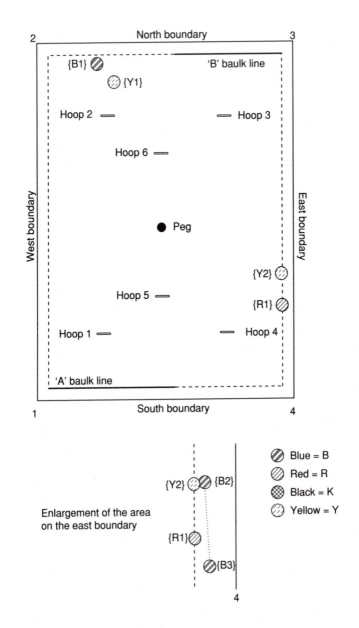

Fig. 22: Using a rush to create a break

EXERCISE

Place the balls as described three paragraphs above, giving yourself the rush towards red from near hoop two. See if you can run hoop three using red.

Problem 2

You are ROY and it is the start of your turn. Red has a perfect rush towards hoop four (its hoop) from near corner one. Black is in corner two, blue is one yard in front of hoop four. What do you do? The hoops required by the other balls may be assumed to have no significance in this problem.

How to use croquet strokes to create breaks

The rush is useful in creating breaks, but the croquet stroke is essential. To show how important the croquet stroke is, each type of shot is considered and examples of its use given. Refer back to Chapter 4 if necessary.

The drive shot

This is the shot that you should use whenever possible because it is the easiest to play and the most predictable. Use it when you are approaching your hoop from about a yard in front. By doing so you will send your ball the two feet needed to get a foot in front of your hoop, whilst the croqueted ball is sent forward about eight feet. When you have run your hoop, the other ball is waiting to be roqueted again. Not only that, you may well have a good rush to somewhere helpful.

Be on the look-out for rushes that give you useful break-making drive shots. An example can be found in the solution to Problem 1.

The roll shot

The need to play a roll shot often indicates a previous poor shot. If you fail to get a good rush to your hoop and end up five yards to the side instead of one yard in front, then a roll shot will be necessary.

There are, however, situations where a roll is the right shot. One of these is where you have made a roquet a long way from your hoop. You do not consider it worth while attempting the hoop, so you roll both balls to positions near the hoop and leave yourself a good rush for your next turn.

Another time when a roll is useful is if you are taking croquet from your ball in the middle of the lawn and wish to retire to a boundary with both of them.

You would also play a roll shot approach to a hoop that you were correctly in front of if you happened to want a rush backwards after running your hoop – perhaps to get to your ball on the boundary behind you. An example of this type of approach will be seen in Chapter 6 under two-ball breaks.

You can see from the above that the roll shot is used more often for recovery or safety than for break-building. Having said that, there are lots of times when recovery or safety shots are required, so practise your rolls!

The stop shot

Play a stop shot if your rush was too good and you are taking croquet from one foot in front of your hoop instead of one yard. That way you will still be able to get the croqueted ball a reasonable distance past your hoop.

A stop shot is also a good ploy if you wish to send the croqueted ball to a useful position, while keeping your ball near another one.

The take-off shot

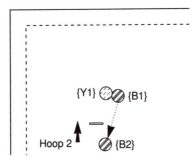

Fig. 23: Approaching a hoop from behind

Use a take-off shot to get in front of your hoop if you have rushed the roqueted ball the wrong side of your hoop, as in fig. 23. By doing this you will still have a ball waiting for you when you have run the hoop. You will not have much say in the position of the croqueted ball as a take-off leaves it almost where it lies. That is the penalty for not getting the rush right!

A take-off shot should also be used when you *want* the croqueted ball to remain where it is. For example: you are trying for hoop two. There is another ball already at hoop two. You are taking croquet from a ball at hoop three. You will want to leave the ball at hoop three where it is so that you can use it after running hoop two. So you play a take-off.

Play a take-off when you cannot send the croqueted ball anywhere useful. Such a situation might be if you were taking croquet from corner three and wished to reach a ball waiting at your hoop two. Any attempt at a roll over that distance is almost certainly doomed.

Opportunities for creating a break

Look out for:

● An opponent's balls left conveniently near your hoop. Try to avoid doing the same thing yourself!

● Opportunities to get a rush on one ball by taking off from another.

● Opportunities to create two-, three- and four-ball breaks. A two-ball break is created simply by getting a rush to your hoop. A three- or four-ball break is created by spotting croquet shots which set up the conditions described in the next sections. The solutions to both Problems 1 and 2 create three-ball breaks.

EXERCISE

Problem 3

Begin with the same situation as in Problem 2 except that the black ball is now one yard due east of hoop one. How would you achieve the following: yellow in front of hoop five, black near the peg, blue as yet untouched and red in a position to roquet blue?

The two-ball break

This is a break using your ball plus one other. The other ball may be your own or the opponent's. It is the easiest break to set up because all you need is a rush to each hoop, but it is the hardest to maintain because of the accuracy required.

Fig. 24 shows a two-ball break from hoop three to hoop five, starting with

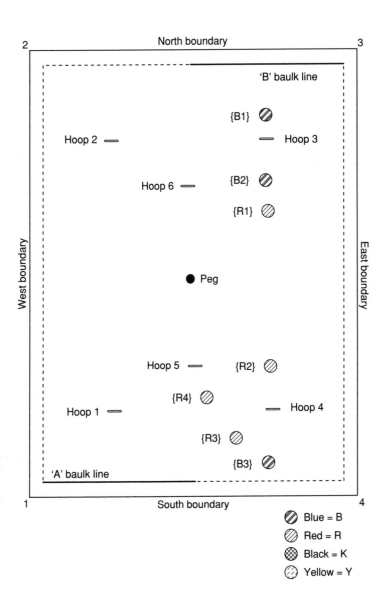

Fig. 24: A two-ball break

your ball in front of hoop three and the other ball beyond it. The letters and figures in curly brackets refer to those on the diagram. Only the key ball positions have been shown, to keep the diagram clearer. Your ball is blue {B1}, the other is red {R1}.

Here is the shot sequence:

1   Run hoop three getting a rush towards hoop four {B2}.

2   Rush red in front of hoop four {R2}.

3   Take croquet. In the croquet stroke put red beyond hoop four and a little to the right {R3}, while putting blue in front of hoop four.

4   Run hoop four getting a rush to hoop five {B3}.

5   Rush red to hoop five {R4}.

6   Take croquet. In the croquet stroke put red beyond hoop five . . .

The general principle of a two-ball break is to run your hoop and get a rush to the next one.

The sequence is quite easy to follow, but is very hard to execute. This is because the two-ball break relies on very accurate rushing, very good croquet stroke placing and very good control when running hoops.

EXERCISE

Set up the balls in the initial positions shown in fig. 24. Follow the sequence and try to run hoops three, four and five. As before, try to get each shot exactly as shown in the book. Make three attempts and if you still have not succeeded, carry on, noting that particular shot for practice.

Problem 4

How might this break be modified if yellow was on the south boundary, directly behind hoop four?

The three-ball break

This is a break using your ball plus two others, which may be your own or the opponent's. Fig. 25 (opposite) shows a three-ball break from hoop three to hoop five, starting with your ball in front of hoop three, one ball beyond hoop three and one ball in front of hoop four. Your ball is blue {B1}, red is as before {R1} and yellow is in front of hoop four {Y1}.

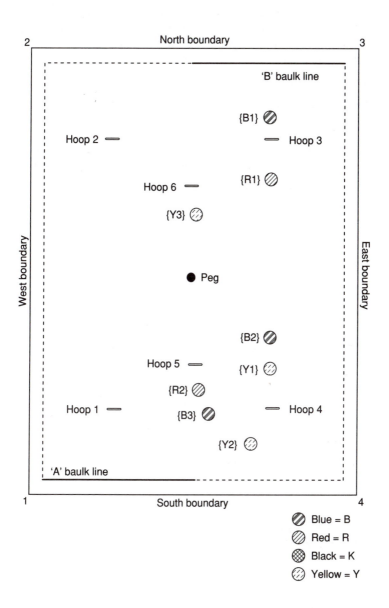

Fig. 25: A three-ball break

One new term occurs in the sequence: *pioneer*. A pioneer is a ball which is sent to your next hoop but one, ready and waiting for you when you get there. In the break you continually create new pioneers, while going to old or previous ones.

Here is the shot sequence:

1 Run hoop three.

2 Roquet red.

3 Take croquet. In the croquet stroke, send red in front of hoop five as a new pioneer {R2}, while putting blue close to yellow, the old pioneer {B2}.

4 Roquet yellow, rushing it to perfect position if necessary.

5 Take croquet. In the croquet stroke put yellow beyond hoop four {Y2}, while putting blue in front of hoop four.

6 Run hoop four.

7 Roquet yellow.

8 Take croquet. In the croquet stroke, send yellow in front of hoop six as a new pioneer {Y3}, while putting blue close to red, the old pioneer {B3}.

9 Roquet red . . .

The general principle of a three-ball break is to run your hoop, roquet a ball, then play a croquet stroke creating a new pioneer while getting in position to roquet the old one.

EXERCISE

Set up the balls in the initial positions shown in fig. 25. Follow the sequence and try to run hoops three, four and five.

Problem 5

What could you try that would make the break easier without adding to the risk of a breakdown? The answer does not involve the use of the fourth ball.

The four-ball break

This is a break using your ball plus all the others. It is the hardest break to set up because all of the balls have to be placed in the correct positions, but the simplest to maintain because once the balls are in position the shots are much easier.

Fig. 26 on page 70 shows a four-ball break from hoop three to hoop five, starting with your ball in front of hoop three, one ball beyond hoop three, one ball in front of hoop four and one ball by the peg. Your ball is blue {B1}, red and yellow are as before {R1} {Y1}, while black is near the peg {K1}.

One new term occurs in the sequence: *pivot*. A pivot is a ball which stays near the peg during a four-ball break.

Here is the shot sequence:

1 Run hoop three.

2 Roquet red.

3 Take croquet. In the croquet stroke, send red in front of hoop five as a new pioneer {R2}, while putting blue close to black, the pivot {B2}.

4 Roquet black.

5 Take croquet. Take-off to yellow, the old pioneer {B3}.

6 Roquet yellow, rushing it to perfect position if necessary.

7 Take croquet. In the croquet stroke put yellow beyond hoop four {Y2}, while putting blue in front of hoop four.

8 Run hoop four.

9 Roquet yellow.

10 Take croquet. In the croquet stroke, send yellow in front of hoop six as a new pioneer {Y3}, while putting blue close to black, the pivot {B4}.

11 Roquet black.

12 Take croquet. Take-off to red, the old pioneer {B5}.

13 Roquet red . . .

A four-ball break is very similar to a three-ball break. Pioneers are created and used in exactly the same way. Your ball, however, uses the pivot ball as an intermediate stop on the way to the old pioneer. The advantage of this is that having run a hoop and made the subsequent roquet, you only have one ball which needs to be sent accurately. This is the new pioneer. Your ball only has to stop somewhere near the pivot.

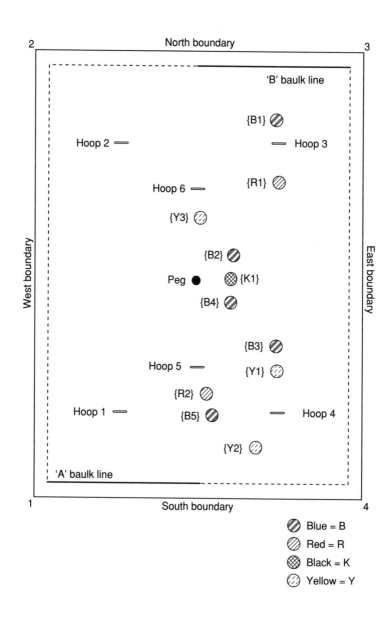

Fig. 26: A four-ball break

You then have a simple take-off shot from the pivot to get good position on the old pioneer.

EXERCISE

Set up the balls in the initial positions shown in fig. 26. Follow the sequence and try to run hoops three, four and five.

Problem 6

In the croquet stroke which was to have sent red in front of hoop five, you play a bad shot. Red only goes as far as the peg. Blue finishes one foot from black (the pivot) with a rush towards yellow. What could you do to restore the four-ball break?

The innings

When a player plays a turn in such a manner that control of the situation belongs to, and remains with, him or her, that player is said to 'have the innings'.

When you start your turn your aim is always to retain the innings if you have it, or to get the innings if you do not have it.

How to keep the innings

'End your turn with your balls united and those of your opponent separated.' This aspect of the game has given rise to many of the misconceptions about croquet, mentioned in Chapter 1. There are a few croquet players even today who believe that keeping one's opponent separated is the only important thing in the game. Hoop running comes a poor second to them and then only one at a time. Breaks are unheard of – much too dangerous! Sadly, new players are often beaten and disillusioned by these people because they do not have the experience to combat such play. If you should have this misfortune, shrug your shoulders and console yourself that few play like this.

So what is the difference between dull, negative play, and proper retention of the innings? Well, you can give your opponent long, difficult shots *and* be aggressive by putting one or both of his or her balls by your next or next-but-one hoops. It is not possible to be precise about this because much depends on the state of play – whose clip is where, etc.

You do not have to do this every time, indeed it may not be possible, but if you *are* separating your opponent, try to be constructive about it.

Do not leave double targets. This is very easy to forget if you are trying to end your turn with a rush for yourself. If you cannot get a rush without leaving a double target, consider leaving a rush for near where you think your opponent may join up. If you have left an aggressive leave as described above, make your rush point towards the ball that the opponent really does not want to move. Now he/she will either have to move it or else put the other ball in a corner. Either way, you keep control.

Make *guarded leaves*. A guarded leave is one where your balls are positioned in such a way that if your opponent shoots and misses, you can roquet the ball that has just missed and make a three-ball break from it. The classic guarded leave points are those which are about three yards diagonally inside the court from each corner towards the hoop that you wish to run. So, say you are trying for hoop two. The guarded leave point is three yards in from corner two. Your opponent shoots and misses. Roquet this ball and in the croquet stroke send it to hoop three, getting a rush on your other ball (which is waiting by hoop two) and thereby making a three-ball break. A guarded leave can be seen in fig. 21 {R5}{Y2}.

EXERCISE

Set up the balls in the guarded leave position described above and obtain a three-ball break by using a ball which is assumed to have just shot and missed. There is no need to run any hoops, just get a break set up. Try the same for the other corners.

Problem 7

Where is the guarded leave point for hoop five?

How to get the innings

The main thing to remember if you do not have the innings is – be patient. It is all too easy to panic when you have not taken croquet for about six turns and your opponent has made four hoops. You then make wild shots and give the game away. The game is not over until one person has pegged out both balls. I have seen a championship match in which one player had made all hoops and pegged out one ball, missing with the other, while his opponent had not scored a single hoop. The opponent then made a roquet and played two all-the-way-round three-ball breaks, to win the game.

The types of shot to play and whether to shoot or not are discussed in detail in the next section.

_____ What to look for when _____ you walk on court

When it is your turn to play, you must have a clear idea about which are the right sort of things to do and which are not. Sometimes the choice is quite easy. Your opponent breaking down at your hoop, leaving you an easy roquet is one example of an easy choice. Sometimes the choice is more difficult – should you take a shot that will give you an easy break if you are successful, but which will give your opponent an equally easy break if you fail? This section gives you some guidelines. Remember, though, the possible combinations of play are endless and what might be the right thing to do for one situation is wrong for another. This is as it should be. If the game became predictable it would be boring.

You should have been watching your opponent carefully. Therefore, when you walk on court, you know the state of play exactly. If for some reason you do not, find out what it is before doing anything. You can normally see the situation clearly by looking at the position of the clips and balls. If there is still any query, ask your opponent. You cannot of course ask your opponent what he or she intends to do next turn!

You will remember from Chapter 4 that there are four choices available to you when you have a continuation stroke after a croquet stroke or after running a hoop. There are similar choices when you play the first stroke of a turn (though, of course, scattering another ball does not apply at the start of a turn because as soon as you hit another ball you have roqueted it).

(a) To roquet a ball

You will then play a croquet shot.

If you are joined up, or have been left a simple roquet on an opponent's ball, then this is an easy choice and you will definitely take this option.

Before you do so, consider the rush. Would a rush help you, and if so, how hard should the rush be? Would it be better not to play a hard rush and instead play a take-off somewhere? Is the apparently obvious ball to play with the right one? It is very easy to think 'Ah, I have a rush with black to black's hoop. Black is the ball to play', ignoring two balls conveniently placed to give an easy break of two hoops or more with blue. The solution to Problem 3 is an example of this.

If you are not joined up, things get more tricky. There is a very useful little question to ask yourself before taking any shot: 'If I am successful with this shot, what benefits will I gain from it? If I fail, what benefits will my opponent gain?'. This question applies particularly when attempting difficult roquets, but can often be asked in other situations. It may stop you from taking suicidal shots which gain you almost nothing if you make a roquet but which give your opponent a three hoop break, or more, if you miss.

If your opponent has left one of your balls near one of his or her hoops, you should move it. If both your balls have been left at an opponent's hoops, move the one which gives your opponent the easiest break.

If you are left with one ball on the boundary and one in the middle of the lawn, move the one in the middle of the lawn.

If joining up (see option (c)), even widely, looks as though it would make things too easy for your opponent, consider shooting at one of your opponent's balls. The best of this type of shot is what is known as a *free shot*. This is one where you shoot hard, so that if you miss your ball carries on to end up harmlessly on a boundary a long way away.

If you do not have a free shot, see if you have a double target. Such a target considerably increases the chance of making a roquet. However, it does not make it certain! A double target 20 yards away is not going to be hit much more often than a single ball.

If you do not have a free shot or a double target, you might have a *safe shot*. A safe shot is one where even if you miss and land near your opponent, the opponent cannot do much with the situation.

(b) To run a hoop

As you will recall from Chapter 4, this is not very common at the start of a turn but it can happen. Running a hoop gives you an extra shot.

1 A croquet set

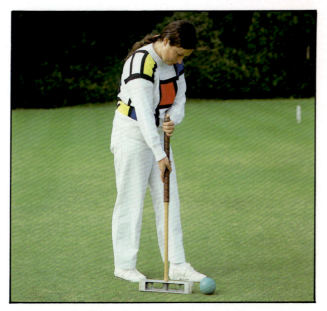

2 Side style stance with standard grip

3   Centre style stance with standard close hands grip

4   Centre style stance with Irish grip

5 Centre style stance with Solomon grip

6 The backswing

7 The strike

8 The follow-through

9 Running a hoop

10 Croquet stroke approaching hoop

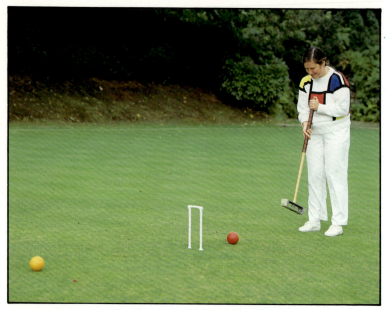

11 Croquet stroke final ball positions

12 Roll shot hand positions

13 Roll shot stance

14 Roll shot just after impact

15 Stop shot stance

16 Stop shot at point of impact

You will then play option (a), (b) or (c), depending on the situation having run the hoop.

If you have been left smack in front of your hoop, then usually you run it. Don't however take on a very difficult shot, particularly if the hoop in question is also your opponent's, or one of your opponent's balls is nearby. Also, if your other ball is within easy roqueting distance of your opponent, running the hoop and then not having an easy roquet yourself is a bad idea.

(c) To take position somewhere

If either making a roquet or running a hoop are not possible, or to attempt them would be too dangerous, either join up or go somewhere safe.

You then have no more shots.

If your opponent is joined up and you are not, do not join up too closely yourself. If you do, you give your opponent an easy pair of balls with which to get a rush (like the tice hit at the beginning of this chapter). Instead, give yourself a *wide join*. To create a wide join position your ball so that it is at a distance from which you would expect to hit most, but not all, of the time. Five yards is a typical figure, but this of course varies with individual ability.

Finally, if none of the above seems like a good idea, then look for the safest corner or boundary and retire to it. The safest place is where you are a long way from your opponent and his or her hoops. Occasionally there just isn't anywhere safe. Then you have to be bold, go for the best shot available and hope that you hit it!

EXERCISE

Problem 8

As befits the final problem, this is a big one!

Set up the balls and clips as follows (fig. 27 on page 76). Yellow is one yard north-east of hoop two, with its clip on hoop one. Red is three feet from yellow with a rush to hoop two, and its clip on hoop two. Blue is halfway between hoops three and four, its clip on hoop two. Black is one yard in from the 'A' baulk (two yards in from the boundary), slightly to one side of hoop one, with its clip on hoop one. Blue and yellow are hidden by hoop six. Black and yellow are hidden by hoop two. All other balls are clear.

1 If it is ROY's turn, what are the options? For each option, answer the

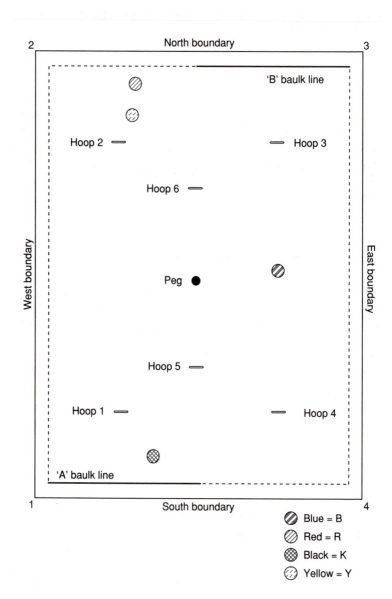

Fig. 27: Problem 8

question 'If I am successful with this shot, what benefits will I gain from it? If I fail, what benefits will my opponent gain?'.

2 Same problem, but now assume that it is BOB's turn.

Try out each situation, giving yourself success first, then failure. See if your estimation of the benefits/losses are justified.

All of the exercises given in this book have been designed to be played individually if you want (or have) to, although it is often helpful to have others around. This final exercise can also be played individually if no-one is available, but it is much better played in twos because you then have to start thinking about an opponent's ability to play as well as your own. If you do play in pairs, pretend to be BOB or ROY alternately to get more practice.

Conclusion

This has been a long chapter and many new ideas have been presented. Don't worry if you didn't understand everything the first time through. You are certainly not expected to be able to do everything. This will take time and a fair amount of practice. When you do have a good understanding, you will be well on your way to becoming a competent croquet player.

You should now be in a position to play a complete game of croquet except for the finish. That is the subject of the next chapter.

Solutions to problems

You will have noticed that in this chapter things are much less precise. There is talk of 'increase the chance' and 'safest place'. This is because each situation described depends on the strokes working correctly. Often they work partly. Often one ball goes the right way but the other does not. The solutions below also rely on everything happening as intended. If all the shots described go exactly as planned, the solution will work. If they do not, it still might work but will be more difficult. So do not think that these solutions are model answers that offer the perfect way to play. You may well see an equally effective solution, even a better one. Well done if you do!

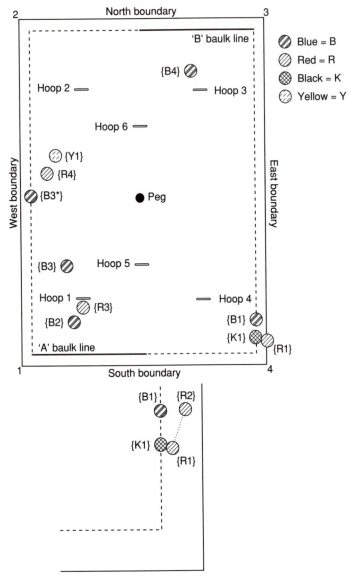

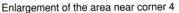

Enlargement of the area near corner 4

Fig. 28: Solution 1 – continuing the break after hoop two

Solution 1 (fig. 28)

How might the above break be modified so that hoop three could be run in the same break?

Instead of taking off from blue {B3} to yellow, play a croquet stroke which sends the blue to hoop three {B4} and puts your ball to a rush position on yellow {R4}. Things would be even better if you had obtained a rush on blue at {B3} to near the west boundary {B3*}. Your croquet shot is then a straight drive rather than an angled part-roll.

Solution 2

You are ROY and it is the start of your turn. Red has a perfect rush towards hoop four (its hoop) from near corner one. Black is in corner two, blue is one yard in front of hoop four. What do you do? The position of all other clips may be assumed to have no bearing on this problem.

Do not take the rush to hoop four. Instead, rush yellow to the east boundary beyond hoop four. In the croquet stroke, play a half roll, sending yellow to hoop five and red to blue.

You have now put the balls in positions which are described as a three-ball break. The three-ball break is very useful and is described in detail on page 66.

Solution 3 (fig. 29)

Begin with the same situation as in Problem 2 except that the black ball is now one yard due east of hoop one. How would you achieve the following: yellow in front of hoop five, black near the peg, blue as yet untouched and red in a position to roquet blue?

Rush yellow a couple of yards {Y2}. In the croquet stroke, send yellow to hoop five {Y3}, getting a rush to the peg on black {R2}. Rush black to near the peg {K2}. In the croquet stroke, take-off to blue {R3}.

You have now put the balls in positions which are described as a four-ball break. The four-ball break is the most useful break you can have and is described in detail on page 68.

Solution 4 (fig. 30)

How might the above break be modified if yellow was on the south boundary, directly behind hoop four?

When approaching hoop four, play your croquet stroke so that red is sent

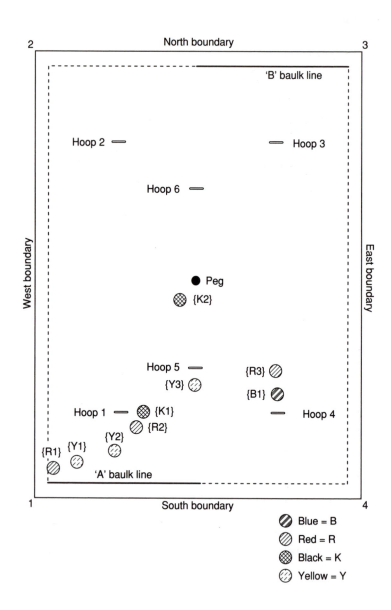

Fig. 29: Solution 3 – positioning balls for a break

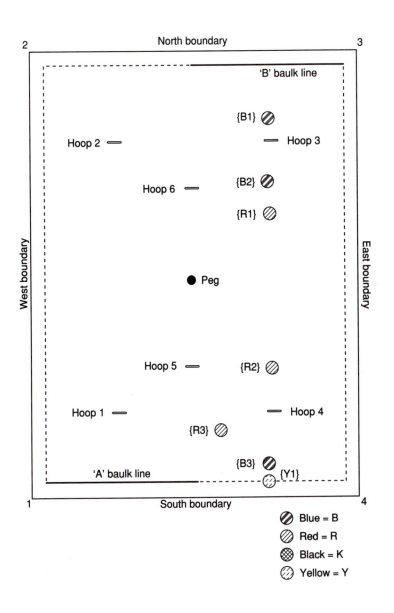

Fig. 30: Solution 4 – a modified two-ball break

at an angle of about 45 degrees to the right and about a yard beyond the hoop {R3}. Run hoop four fairly firmly so that your ball stops near yellow. Roquet yellow. In the croquet stroke, send yellow to hoop six, getting a rush on red to hoop five.

Note 1: When you run hoop four, if your ball continues off court, it is replaced on the yard line and you continue your turn.

Note 2: If your ball does not go off court but stops in the yard line area, your continuation shot is played from where it lies – it is not replaced on the yard line (see earlier in this chapter under 'How to make a break').

Note 3: If your ball runs the hoop and roquets yellow in the same stroke, you take croquet immediately. This is true whenever you run a hoop and make a roquet in the same stroke. The continuation stroke for running the hoop is lost.

If you succeed in the rush, you have created another three-ball break.

Solution 5 (fig. 31)

What could you try that would make the break easier without adding to the risk of a breakdown? The answer does not involve the use of the fourth ball.

The answer to this problem was given as part of the answer to Problem 1. If you can obtain a rush on the other ball having run a hoop, you will be able to play much easier croquet strokes. In the diagram, which is a partial repeat of fig. 25, the rush on red to a point near yellow {R1*} gives a much better shot than from its original position {R1}.

Solution 6

In the croquet stroke which was to have sent red in front of hoop five, you play a bad shot. Red only goes as far as the peg. Blue finishes one foot from black (the pivot) with a rush towards yellow. What could you do to restore the four-ball break?

Rush black to a few yards past yellow. In the croquet stroke, send black to hoop five and blue near yellow.

Solution 7

Where is the guarded leave point for hoop five?

Three yards from the south boundary, in front of hoop five. This solution is only true if your opponent's balls are somewhere separated towards

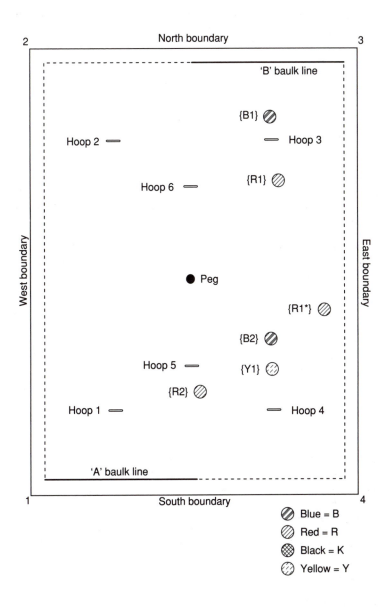

Fig. 31: Solution 5 – an improved three-ball break

the north boundary. If they are not then near corner one or four, as appropriate, gives a partially guarded leave.

Solution 8

1 *If it were ROY's turn, what are the options? In each case, how do the questions 'If I am successful with this shot, what benefits will I gain from it? If I fail, what benefits will my opponent gain?' get answered?*

Red playing

(a) Going safe or shooting at anything other than yellow is daft, so these choices can be ignored.

(b) Shooting at yellow gives a very good chance of making hoop two and a very good chance of a safe leave, even a guarded leave afterwards. There is little the opponent can gain from this specific shot. This is a good safe choice.

Yellow playing

(a) Going safe or shooting at anything other than red is as daft as it was for red at yellow, so these choices can be ignored.

(b) Shooting at red gives a possible chance of making hoop one off black by playing take-offs to blue, then black. Red is left near hoop two, giving the potential for a four-ball break since blue is near the middle. However, black is only two yards in from the boundary and it is a long journey from red. The benefits are great if you succeed but potentially dangerous if you fail (depending of course on how you fail). This is an adventurous and slightly hazardous choice.

2 *If it were BOB's turn, what are the options? In each case, how do the questions 'If I am successful with this shot, what benefits will I gain from it? If I fail, what benefits will my opponent gain?' get answered?*

Black playing

(a) Moving black seems reasonable if you think that choice (b) above would still be made by ROY, even if blue were moved. Going into corner four is very defensive, and gives no chance of a turn. It is however very safe. The benefit to you is nil, but the loss to the opponent is a potential three-ball break. This is a defensive choice.

(b) Shooting at blue gives a partially free shot, going off along the east boundary, yet giving the chance of a roquet. The benefit to you if you hit is a long shot at a break by taking off to red and yellow, using them to get a rush to hoop one. You have also separated your opponent. The benefit to the opponent if you miss is a possible break chance using red. This is a calculated risk choice.

(c) The yellow/red part double is 30 yards away and gives no better chance of a break if you hit and a moderate chance for your opponent to pick up a four-ball break if you miss. From black's point of view, ROY has a partially guarded leave. This shot gains little and could lose much. It is a bad choice.

(d) Trying to run hoop one is likely to result in you bouncing off the hoop, leaving ROY an easy three-ball break. It is a bad choice.

Blue playing

(a) Moving blue seems reasonable if you think that yellow choice (b) above would not be made by ROY. Going into corner four is very defensive, and gives no chance of a turn but it does provide a chance for black to join wide next time, and it is very safe. The benefit to you is little, the loss to the opponent little. This is a long-term defensive choice.

(b) Shooting at black puts two balls near hoop one if you miss, but a chance to take-off to two balls at your hoop if you hit. The benefit to you is a three-ball break chance. The benefit to your opponent is an excellent three-ball break chance. This is a reckless choice.

(c) Joining wide with black gives virtually the same chance of a three-ball break to ROY without even the long shot at a roquet that (b) gave you. This is a thoughtless and foolish choice.

(d) Shooting at red gives an excellent chance of a three-ball break if you hit and an equally excellent chance for your opponent to pick up a three-ball break if you miss. From blue's point of view, ROY has a guarded leave. This shot could gain much and could lose much. It is an aggressive and dangerous choice.

So there are the choices. Nothing is certain, no option is guaranteed. I know my own skills and would have my own preferred choice, but other players could well choose differently. Sometimes the choices are easy, sometimes very hard, but each time a ball is moved, the choices alter. Croquet is a fascinating game!

6

— FINISHING A GAME —

——— The rules for pegging out ———

It has already been noted in previous chapters that until a ball has run all of its hoops, it can neither be pegged out nor cause another ball to be pegged out. Although it would be perfectly legal for ROY to peg out yellow in one turn, and red in another, a better way is to wait until both balls have run all hoops. Then, by some means (discussed in a moment), ROY, here playing red, arranges for the final roquet to be made on yellow, rushing it near to the peg. With the croquet stroke, yellow is pegged out and removed from the court. Finally, with the continuation stroke, red is pegged out.

However, a few oddities can arise as follows:

- If ROY rushes yellow towards the peg (with the idea of finishing as described above) and yellow hits the peg, his turn immediately finishes. This is because a rushed ball can score a point against the peg just as it can when it is rushed through a hoop (a rush peel). Since the peg point has been scored, yellow has been pegged out. It is removed from the game and ROY has nothing from which to take croquet!

- If, in the croquet stroke in which yellow is pegged out, yellow bounces off the peg and moves red, or any other ball, nothing is replaced. Yellow is still removed and ROY's continuation shot played. If you spot that this is going to happen in your game, let it. Do not try to stop the collision, as it is a legitimate part of the game.

- If, in the croquet stroke, both balls hit the peg, both are pegged out and the game ends.

- It is perfectly legitimate to peg out any opponent's ball which has also run all of its hoops. This is a tactical move (see the section later on pegging out tactics). In the example above, ROY could peg out blue if it had run all of its hoops.

— Pegging out from a two-ball break —

In this and also in the three/four-ball break situations which follow, the break will start at hoop five, with your taking croquet in front of hoop five. Whether this is the start of your turn or whether you are in the middle of a longer break does not matter for the purpose of the discussion. It is also assumed throughout that your other ball has run all of its hoops and can therefore be pegged out.

You are ROY playing with red {R1} (see fig. 32 over the page).

(a) The other ball is yours {Y1}

In the croquet stroke, put yellow about three-quarters of the way to the peg {Y2} while putting red in front of hoop five. Run hoop five, getting a rush for hoop six on yellow {R2}. Rush yellow in front of hoop six {Y3}. Take croquet and in the croquet stroke, put yellow level with hoop six and to the side by a few inches {Y4}, while putting red in front of hoop six. Run hoop six by about three feet, getting a rush on yellow towards the peg {R3}. Rush yellow to near the peg {Y5} and peg out as described above.

(b) The other ball is an opponent's ball

Play hoop five as described above. For hoop six, in the croquet stroke, put blue in such a position that when you have run hoop six {R3}, you have a rush on blue {B4} to your *other* ball {Y1}. Take-off from blue to your other ball so that you have a rush towards the peg. Peg out as described above.

‑ Pegging out from a three-ball break ‑

(a) Your other ball is the one at hoop five

You are therefore taking croquet from yellow in front of hoop five {R1}{Y1} and blue is in front of hoop six {B1} (see fig. 33 on page 89). In the croquet stroke, put yellow about three-quarters of the way to the peg {Y2} while putting red in front of hoop five. Run hoop five, getting a rush

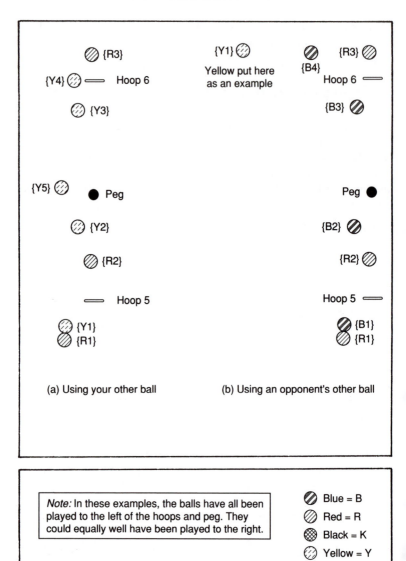

(a) Using your other ball   (b) Using an opponent's other ball

Note: In these examples, the balls have all been played to the left of the hoops and peg. They could equally well have been played to the right.

Blue = B
Red = R
Black = K
Yellow = Y

Fig. 32: Pegging out from a two-ball break

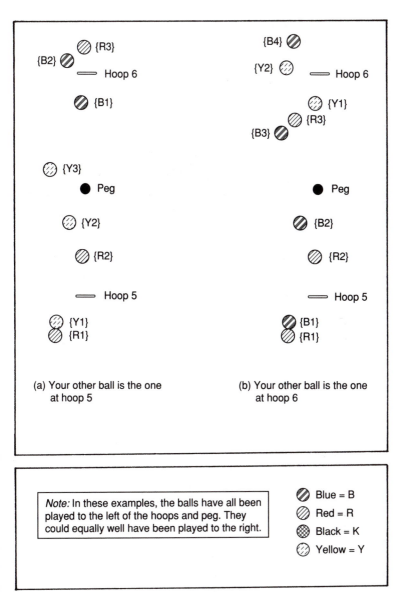

(a) Your other ball is the one at hoop 5

(b) Your other ball is the one at hoop 6

Note: In these examples, the balls have all been played to the left of the hoops and peg. They could equally well have been played to the right.

Blue = B
Red = R
Black = K
Yellow = Y

Fig. 33: Pegging out from a three-ball break

to near the peg on yellow {R2}. Rush yellow near to the peg {Y3}. Take croquet and take-off to blue at hoop six. Roquet blue. Take croquet and in the croquet stroke, put blue a few feet beyond hoop six and to the side by about a foot {B2}, while putting red in front of hoop six. Run hoop six by about a yard, getting a rush on blue towards yellow {R3}. This rush is not too critical. Take-off for yellow near the peg and peg out.

(b) Your other ball is the one at hoop six

You are therefore taking croquet from blue in front of hoop five {R1}{B1}, and yellow is in front of hoop six {Y1}. In the croquet stroke, put blue about three-quarters of the way to the peg {B2} while putting red in front of hoop five. Run hoop five, getting a rush to near yellow on blue {R2}. Rush blue near to yellow {B3}. Take croquet and in the croquet stroke send blue two yards beyond hoop six {B4} and red near yellow {R3}. Roquet yellow. Take croquet and in the croquet stroke, put yellow to the left of hoop six by about a foot and just beyond it {Y2}, while putting red in front of hoop six. Run hoop six and roquet blue. Take-off, getting a rush to near the peg with yellow and peg out.

— Pegging out from a four-ball break —

(a) Your other ball is not the one at hoop six

You are therefore either taking croquet from yellow in front of hoop five, or yellow is the pivot ball. Blue and black occupy the other positions of the break. In either case, continue the four-ball break, making sure that yellow is left near the peg. Run hoop six and take-off either directly or via the opponent's balls for yellow near the peg and peg out.

(b) Your other ball is the one at hoop six

You are therefore taking croquet from blue or black in front of hoop five and yellow is in front of hoop six. The method of play is the same as for the three-ball break (b) except that you have an extra ball to use.

EXERCISES

Set up each of the six situations described above and successfully peg out both balls.

You should be able to achieve a peg out about 50 per cent of the time.

—— The tactics of pegging out ——

Ideally, you will be able to complete the last hoops and peg out as described above and your opponent will get no more chances. When this does not happen and you are left with two clips on the peg, some strategy is called for.

(a) You have the innings

You should be attempting to leave your opponent widely separated, while you have a rush to the peg. The difficulty is to achieve this but not leave a double target. If you do leave a double target, your opponent will shoot; see (b) below.

If your opponent is separated and you don't have a rush to the peg, roll up close and peg your ball out. You then hope that your opponent misses so that you can peg the other ball out next turn!

(b) You do not have the innings

If both your opponent's balls are for the peg, then something needs to be done quickly. There is a very useful rule here.

If in your estimation your opponent is certain to finish next turn, try for the shortest roquet shot available to you. If your opponent may go out but it is not certain, join up.

However, if your opponent leaves you a double target, shoot for it anyway, unless your balls are quite close to each other.

(c) Pegging out an opponent's ball

Sometimes you will find that your opponent has got as far as the peg with one ball, while the other has some way to go. If you then reach the peg with one ball of your own, it can be useful to peg out the opponent's ball but not your own. The opponent then has nothing to join up with and must either shoot at you to make a hoop or try to get round without being able to roquet anything.

Tactics for the player of the two balls
Stay together, but do not leave any easy targets for the single ball. Do not use the opponent's ball unless an obvious three-ball break can be constructed or you have to move it out of the way. Remember that if you do not move the single ball, you can hide behind hoops without conceding a lift shot (described on page 108).

Tactics for the player of the single ball
Be aggressive. Shoot for your opponent every time unless to do so and miss is absolute suicide. If shooting is too dangerous, lurk on a boundary near your opponent's next hoop. If your opponent becomes separated or wired, take position in front of your hoop.

You are now in a position to play a complete game of croquet. The next chapter looks at how to put time limits on a game and how to even out different playing standards by handicapping.

7

SCORING AND HANDICAPS

───── **Scoring and timing games** ─────

A game which is played to its conclusion no matter how long it takes will finish when one player (one pair in doubles) pegs out both balls. This means that the winner will have scored fourteen points – six hoops plus the peg for each ball. The loser will have scored less than this. The winner is therefore said to have won by fourteen points to X. X is the score of the loser.

Another way of expressing the result is to take X from fourteen and say that the winner has won by plus Y, where Y equals fourteen minus X.

Example
BOB pegs out both balls when ROY has clips on hoop four and peg. BOB has scored fourteen points, ROY has scored nine points. BOB has won by fourteen to nine (or BOB has won by plus five).

Timed games

Because untimed games can take a long time (the author knows personally of one game which took seven hours), players can agree on a time limit before starting. If there is a winner before time is up, the scoring is as above. If not, then each player (or side) adds up the total number of points and the one with the most points wins.

Example

After time ROY has clips on hoops two and six while BOB has clips on hoops one and three. ROY has scored six points, BOB has scored two points. ROY has won by six to two on time (or ROY has won by plus four on time).

The rules on the finish of a timed game are as follows:

1   Players agree on the clock or watch used for timing and the time at which to finish, before the game starts.

2   If there is no-one to watch the clock, the player not in play does the watching.

3   At the exact point when time is up, the watcher calls '*time*'.

4   The player in play when time is called is allowed to finish his or her turn. The opponent then also has one more turn. Unless there is a tied score, the game is over.

5   If there *is* a tie, the game continues until just one more point is scored by a player. That player then wins by plus one on time.

Example

When time is called ROY is in play with yellow and is about to run hoop four. The red clip is on hoop three. ROY runs hoop four with yellow but fails to run hoop five. BOB has one more turn. The black clip is on hoop four, the blue on hoop two. BOB hits in with blue and runs hoops two and three but fails to run hoop four. Both players have now scored six points. It is a tie. Play continues. ROY fails to hit in and BOB runs hoop four with blue.

BOB wins by seven points to six on time (or BOB wins by plus one on time).

A longer game

This book has described a game in which six hoops are run in a single direction by each ball, plus two peg points, giving a fourteen-point game. It is possible to make a longer game by running each hoop in both directions. This gives twelve hoops plus a peg point for each ball making a 26-point game. The route for this longer game is given in fig. 34 on page 104. This version is the one most often played at clubs.

The order of hoops is: hoops one to six as before, then:

one-back (hoop two in the reverse direction),
two-back (hoop one in the reverse direction),
three-back (hoop four in the reverse direction),
four-back (hoop three in the reverse direction),
five-back – called *penultimate* (hoop six in the reverse direction),
six-back – called *rover* (hoop five in the reverse direction),

and finally, the peg.

Readers should note that this longer or full game, as it is known, can take a long time to play, especially on a larger lawn. It is not recommended that you play a full game until you can regularly make breaks of three or four hoops.

Handicaps

It will not be very long, in a family or group of friends, before some players play better than others. This is so with any competitive game. To avoid the better players becoming bored and the less able players frustrated, a handicap system exists which balances abilities. This system allows the weaker player to have a certain number of extra turns, the amount varying according to the difference in ability.

Bisques

An extra turn is called a *bisque* turn and a player opting for such a turn is said to *take a bisque*. The section on page 97 explains how to work out the correct number of bisque turns to be played in any one game. To keep track of the number of bisque turns a player has left, small sticks, called bisques, are stuck into the ground at some convenient point at the edge of the lawn. Any odd sticks will do, paint them white and cut them into pieces about a foot long. Typically about 20 bisques will be enough for a single croquet set.

How to take a bisque

You can take a bisque immediately after the end of your ordinary turn. You must play with the ball that you have just been using – you cannot change to your other ball.

Example 1
You are playing with red. You are trying to run hoop three. Unfortunately

you stick in the hoop. Your turn ends, but you have a bisque. By taking your bisque you can start a new turn immediately and continue through the hoop.

Example 2
You shoot at your opponent on the boundary and just miss. Your ball is replaced on the yard line next to your opponent. Your turn ends, but you have a bisque. By taking your bisque you can start a new turn immediately and roquet your opponent.

The effect of taking a bisque

A bisque is a completely new turn. You should remember this when you take a bisque because it means that you are allowed to roquet all three balls again even though you haven't yet run a hoop.

Example 3
One of your balls, yellow, is in the middle of the lawn, while red is in corner three. With red, which is for hoop one, you shoot at blue (which is close to black near corner two) and hit. With a stop shot you send blue to hoop two. You then roquet black and send it to hoop one. With your continuation shot you put red close to blue (or yellow, it doesn't matter, but blue is closer). Your turn ends, but you have a bisque. Take the bisque and you start a new turn with the balls all laid out in a perfect four-ball break!

Bisque turns may be taken in sequence, so one bisque turn can immediately follow another.

Example 4
Having set up the four-ball break in example 3, you stick in hoop one. If you have several bisques, you can take a second one to continue through hoop one, maintaining the break.

What is my handicap?

The aim of any handicapping system is to give everyone an equal chance of winning. Croquet clubs have an appointed handicapper who tries to achieve this, but friends and families need to have their own system. A suggested system is described next. Note that the scheme is only intended for singles play; it is not really possible to decide individual handicapping in a doubles match.

Start off the system by giving everyone a handicap of ten. After each game, reduce the winner's handicap by one and increase the loser's handicap by one.

Example 5

ROY plays BOB in the first game. They are both ten. ROY beats BOB. ROY's handicap is now nine, BOB's is eleven. The next time they play, BOB will have a bisque advantage over ROY. If BOB wins this time they will both go back to ten. If ROY wins again, the handicaps will be eight and twelve respectively.

After a while, the wins and losses will probably even out as each player reaches his or her correct handicap. At this point it is not a good idea to change both handicaps after every game, but only reduce someone who wins two games in succession or increase someone who loses two games in succession.

If someone is really good and keeps winning even when their handicap reaches 0, just keep going into minus figures. Note that the difference between, say, minus two and twelve is fourteen, not ten.

How many bisques do I get?

There are two ways of calculating the number of bisques.

1   Standard handicap play

In this scheme, the higher handicap player receives bisques equal to the handicap difference of the players. So if ROY is seven and BOB is ten, BOB has three extra bisque turns.

This means that in the very first game, where everyone is ten, play will be level and there are no extra bisque turns for the two players.

Example 5

ROY plays BOB in the first game. They are both ten so play level. ROY beats BOB. ROY's handicap is now nine, BOB's is eleven. The next time they play, BOB will have two extra bisque turns' advantage over ROY. If BOB wins this time they will both go back to ten. If ROY wins again, the handicaps will be eight and twelve respectively and BOB will have four extra bisque turns next time they play.

2   Full bisque handicap play

In this scheme, each player receives bisques equal to his or her handicap.

So if ROY was seven and BOB was ten, ROY would have seven extra bisque turns and BOB would have ten extra bisque turns.

This will mean that in the very first game, each player has ten extra bisque turns.

Example 6
ROY plays BOB in the first game. They are both ten so each has ten extra bisque turns. ROY beats BOB. ROY's handicap is now nine, BOB's is eleven. The next time they play, BOB will have eleven extra bisque turns, while ROY will have nine. If BOB wins this time they will both go back to ten. If ROY wins again, they will have eight and twelve extra bisque turns respectively.

Which is the best scheme?

There are advantages and disadvantages to both schemes.

The standard scheme allows the better player to play without bisques and win on his or her own merits. Apart from the extra turns that the weaker player gets, the game is very close to a non-handicap match. However, it can take a long time to play a game to a conclusion without time limits, as already mentioned. Also, the better player is forced to play more defensively because of the extra turns that the opponent possesses.

The full bisque version allows both players to build breaks and get out of trouble. Constructive play is encouraged due to both sides having extra turns. The game should therefore be quicker. However, it is a more artificial situation as players know they can take risks that they would not take without bisques.

Faults

If a turn stops due to a fault being committed, for example sending a ball off court in a croquet stroke, a bisque can be used to start a new turn.

If bisque(s) are taken in a series of consecutive turns which then turn out to be invalid (for example, hoops scored in the wrong order), any bisques used after the error was committed are restored, but not any used before.

Doubles play

Although doubles play cannot be used to judge singles handicaps, players' handicaps can be used to play handicap doubles games.

For standard handicap doubles play the players of each pair add together their handicaps. The higher handicap side receives half the difference between the totals, rounded up to the nearest whole. Either player of a side may use the bisques.

Example 7
BOB (six) and ROY (five) play BOG (ten) and POW (four) (who normally play with the secondary colours!) in a handicap game.

BOB-ROY's total is eleven, BOG-POW's fourteen. BOG-POW therefore receive half of fourteen minus eleven, which is one and a half. This is rounded up to two.

For full bisque play, each player receives half their normal bisques, rounded up to the nearest whole. Players may only use their own bisques.

Example 8
Same match as example 7. BOB has three bisques, ROY has three bisques, BOG has five bisques and POW has two bisques.

If a player commits a fault and the turn ends, a bisque may be taken to start a new turn but only by the player who committed the fault.

Handicap tactics

This is a topic large enough for a book (see the Bibliography on page 131). Here are a few pointers to start you on the fascinating trail of tactical handicap croquet.

If you have a lot of bisques (six or more), use a couple to set up a four-ball break, plus others as necessary to maintain the break. Do not try this until you have enough skill to fulfil the elements of a four-ball break; see Chapter 5.

If you have a few bisques (three to five), look for situations where you can set up a three or four-ball break with just one bisque, then use others as necessary to maintain the break.

If you have one or two bisques, look for situations where you can set up a three or four-ball break with just one bisque.

Occasionally you should use a bisque defensively to get out of trouble, for example when you have failed to run a hoop and left your opponent a very easy break. However, remember that in a full bisque game, your opponent has bisques as well, so a purely defensive bisque may not be enough.

Do not use bisques for impossible or highly speculative situations, for the result will be a wasted bisque.

When faced with a difficult situation, consider if you can improve it with a bisque. If you can, remember that you can roquet all of the balls again, so you may be able to improve the situation even more than at first seemed possible.

If you have a situation which is possible but difficult by taking a bisque, consider if two bisques taken consecutively will make things easy.

When your opponent has bisques and you do not, do not leave situations that make it easy for him or her. Examples are:

- Leaving your balls near your opponent's hoop.

- Leaving a ball or balls near your opponent's next hoop.

- Leaving your balls in the middle of the lawn.

When your opponent has bisques and you do not, try to leave situations that encourage him or her to use bisques without good effect – in other words, waste them. Examples are:

- Leaving your balls with a rush for your hoop, but a long way from your opponent's hoop.

- Leaving a ball or balls near your hoops, but not your opponent's.

- Leaving your opponent's balls in the middle of the lawn, some way apart.

Doubles handicap tactics

Doubles play is not very different from singles play, but there are a few things to observe:

Discuss with your partner which is the best thing to do, but don't spend ages about it, or the game will get boring.

Having decided what to do, accept what happens, right or wrong. Do not argue about what might have been.

Watch your partner, and forestall any errors, but do not leap on court every two minutes to challenge or discuss play.

You can assist your partner in every way except with the actual shot. So you can line up balls and demonstrate swings, etc.

You should now have a working knowledge of basic croquet. Quite often, unusual points of law will occur in your games. To help with this, the next chapter gives a comprehensive reference guide to the rules of association croquet.

8

THE LAWS OF ——— ASSOCIATION ——— CROQUET

The official laws of croquet are published by the Croquet Association and may be obtained from them; see Appendix 1. They are complex, particularly when dealing with a version called 'advanced croquet'. This chapter is based on the 1989 edition, and rules have been simplified or amended where required. For those readers who possess the laws book and would like to cross-refer to it, this chapter uses the same numbers for the laws. This means that there will be missing numbers where laws that are not relevant to this book are omitted.

——— Guide to the laws ———

The laws are set out in a logical order. They start with a general description of the game, followed by detailed descriptions of specific actions such as roquets, hoop points and so on. Laws relating to things that can go wrong then follow. The final set of laws relates to variations of the standard game.

The list which follows will assist you in finding specific topics.

Topic and related laws

The court and equipment
   1–3

Ordinary singles play   **4–25**

Errors and interference
   26–35

Part 1

The standard court and equipment

1   The standard court

This is a rectangle measuring 35 by 28 yards (32 by 25.6 metres). Where marking (a white line or string) is used, the inner edge is the exact boundary. Fig. 34 shows the measurements for a standard court.

2   Equipment

The peg should be 1½ inches (38mm) wide and 18 inches (450mm) high. It should have a detachable extension to hold clips.

Hoops should be 12 inches (300mm) high and between 3¾ inches (95mm) and 4 inches (100mm) wide.

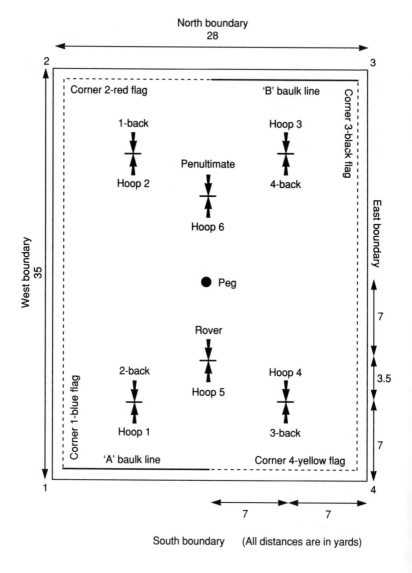

Fig. 34: The standard court

Balls should be 3⅝ inches (92mm) in diameter and weigh one pound (454kg). If they are coloured blue, black, red and yellow, blue/black plays red/yellow. If they are coloured green, brown, pink and white, green/brown plays pink/white. For other colours, the darker two balls play the lighter two.

Clips should be the same colour as the balls used. If no clips are available, painted clothes pegs will often suffice.

3 Court accessories

Flags and corner pegs are not essential to the game, but where provided may be placed as shown in fig. 35.

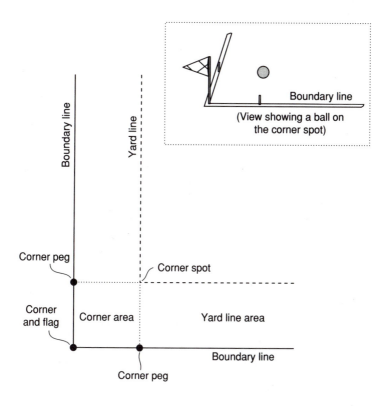

Fig. 35: The corner area

——————— **Part 2** ———————

Ordinary singles play

4   An outline of the game

(a)   This law describes the game generally and is modified by the detailed laws which follow.

(b)   The object of the game is for a player – with both balls – to run all hoops in the correct sequence and then strike the peg.

A ball which has run all hoops but not yet struck the peg is called a rover ball. A rover ball which strikes the peg is then known as a pegged out ball. A pegged out ball is removed from the game. A rover ball can also cause any other rover ball to be pegged out (see law 15).

(c)   The game is played by striking a ball with a mallet (see laws 31 and 32). The player whose turn it is, is known as the striker. The ball he or she strikes is the striker's ball. His or her other ball is the partner ball. The remaining two balls are the opponent's balls.

(d)   Players play alternate turns. At the start of a turn a player chooses which ball to play (see law 8), and must strike only that ball in that turn (see law 28).

If the striker's ball runs a hoop, the striker is entitled to an extra stroke called a continuation stroke (see laws 4g and 21).

If the striker's ball makes a roquet (see law 16), the striker is entitled to two extra strokes. The first is known as a croquet stroke (see laws 4f and 20). It is played after placing the striker's ball in contact with the roqueted ball (see law 19). The second extra stroke is a continuation stroke, as described in 4g.

At the start of a turn the striker's ball may roquet each of the other three balls once only. If, however, a hoop is scored, the three balls may be roqueted once again.

(e)   The score is indicated by the position of the clips. Each clip is placed on the top of the hoop next in order for that ball. When a full game is played (see Chapter 7), the clips are placed on the side of the hoop to indicate the second six hoops.

(f)   In a croquet stroke the other ball must move or shake when the striker's ball is struck. Also, neither ball may go off court (see law 20).

(g) A continuation stroke is played in the same way as is the first stroke of a turn: i.e. a hoop may be run, a roquet made, etc. Continuation strokes are not cumulative, so:

- If a hoop and a roquet are made in the same stroke, croquet is taken and the hoop continuation shot is lost.

- If a roquet is made in a croquet stroke, croquet is taken and the continuation shot is lost.

- If two hoops are run in one stroke, only one continuation shot is allowed.

- If a hoop is made in a croquet stroke, only one continuation shot is allowed.

5   The toss

The winner of the toss may choose either to play first or second, or which colour balls to use. The loser has whichever choice is left.

6   The start of a game

At the start of the game, all four balls are played from any point on the 'A' or 'B' baulk lines. In the first turn the first player will play one of the chosen two balls. In the second turn the second player will do likewise. In the third and fourth turns the third and fourth balls *must* be brought into play. After this, law 4d applies.

7   Ball in play

Law 6 brings balls into play. Balls remain in play until pegged out and are eligible to score points, except under law 9.

8   Election of striker's ball

Law 4d allows the striker to choose a ball to play. This choice is indicated by either moving, lifting or striking a ball.

9   Ball in hand

Any ball is 'in hand' (and is not in play) when it is off court, or when it is in the yard line area at the end of a turn.

Additionally, the striker's ball is in hand when it has made a roquet. *Note:* this means that having made a roquet, the striker's ball cannot then bounce off and score a hoop or the peg, although it can score a point for another ball by peeling it (see laws 14f and 18).

10   Ball off court

A ball is off court when any part of it crosses over the inside edge of the boundary (see law 12).

11   Balls in the yard line area

All balls which do not go off court but end up in the yard line area are immediately placed on the yard line or corner spot as appropriate (see law 12). *Exception:* after a croquet stroke or having run a hoop, the striker's ball is not replaced but played from where it lies.

12   Replacement of balls off court or in the yard line area

Balls are replaced on the yard line at the nearest point to where the ball went off court (or lies if it stopped in the yard line area). If the ball went off, or lies, in the corner area (see fig. 35), it is replaced on the corner spot.

In all cases, if there is a ball already occupying the replacement spot, the striker's ball is replaced in contact with it, on the yard line. The striker chooses which side. Both balls must be on the yard line.

13   Wiring lift

At the start of a turn, if a striker's ball has no clear shot at any other ball, the striker may lift that ball and play it from the 'A' or 'B' baulk. A clear shot means being able to hit any part of the target ball with any part of the striker's ball.

These three conditions must also be met:

● The opponent must have put the striker's ball there.

● The obstruction(s) can only be hoops or the peg, not other balls.

● The striker's ball must not already be touching another ball (see law 16c).

A lift is also given, even when there is a clear shot, provided that the three conditions above are met and either the striker's backswing is impeded by a hoop or peg, or the striker's ball is in the jaws of a hoop.

14   Hoop point

(a)   A ball scores a hoop point by passing through the correct hoop in the correct direction.

(b)   The part of the hoop which faces the striker as he or she is about to run the hoop is called the playing side.

(c)   A ball starts to run a hoop when its leading edge is level with the front of the hoop on the non-playing side. A ball completes the running of a hoop when its trailing edge no longer protrudes on the playing side.

(d)   A ball may run a hoop in more than one turn; i.e. having started to run in one turn, it can complete in another.

(e)   A hoop may be scored in a croquet stroke provided it has not begun to run the hoop when placed for that croquet stroke. See also law 4g.

(f)   A ball other than the striker's ball can be made to score its hoop. This can occur in a croquet stroke (peeling) or in a roquet (rush peeling).

15   Peg point

Only a rover ball may score a peg point. When the point is scored, the ball is removed from the game. A rover ball may croquet or rush another rover ball onto the peg to peg it out. *Note:* In a rush peg out the turn ends because the rushed ball, although roqueted, is removed from the game.

16   Roquet

Definition
A roquet is made when the striker's ball hits one of the other three balls. A croquet stroke (see law 20) is then taken. From the start of a turn each of the three balls may, if desired, be roqueted in turn. If, meanwhile, a hoop is run, all balls roqueted so far may be roqueted again. No ball can be roqueted twice in the same turn unless a hoop is run.

Additional points
(a)   The striker's ball can either make a roquet with a direct hit, or after it has hit a hoop or peg or another ball on which a roquet has already been made.

(b)   If two balls are hit in the same shot, it is the first ball hit which is roqueted.

(c) If, at the start of a turn, the striker elects to play a ball that is in contact with another ball, a roquet is deemed to have been made and the striker takes croquet from that ball immediately.

(d) If there is another ball in the jaws of the striker's hoop, which may be, and is, roqueted, croquet is taken from that ball wherever it is rushed to. No hoop point is scored for the striker's ball even if it then continues through the hoop.

(e) If there is another ball in the jaws of the striker's hoop which has already been roqueted, a hoop point is scored if the striker's ball hits that ball and then continues through the hoop. No roquet is made except under (c) above.

17 Hoop and roquet in the same stroke

If there is a ball the other side of the hoop (clear of the jaws), which is hit as, or after, the striker's ball runs its hoop, hoop and roquet are scored together. Croquet is taken and the hoop continuation shot is lost. To achieve both hoop and roquet, when the striker's ball comes to rest, it must have passed through the hoop. If it has not, the hoop is not run and either croquet is taken if the other ball has not been roqueted before, or the turn ends if it has.

18 Consequences of a roquet

If a roquet is made, the striker's ball (in that stroke) cannot score a hoop or peg point for itself (except under law 17), but can cause other balls to score by knocking them through their hoop (rush peeling) or against the peg if they are rover balls (rush peg out).

19 Placing balls for the croquet stroke

(a) The striker's ball is placed in contact with the roqueted ball but not touching any other ball. It may touch a hoop or the peg but see law 32.

(b) If there are three balls (the striker's ball, the roqueted ball and one other) together on the yard line or in the corner, paragraph (a) applies plus: the third ball is then placed anywhere in contact with the roqueted ball but not in contact with the striker's ball.

(c) If there are four balls (the striker's ball, the roqueted ball and two others) together on the yard line or in the corner, paragraphs (a) and (b) apply plus: the fourth ball is then placed anywhere in contact with any ball except the striker's.

20 Croquet stroke

(a) In a croquet stroke the roqueted ball becomes known as the croqueted ball.

(b) The striker plays a stroke with the balls placed according to law 19 in such a way as to move or shake both balls.

(c) The striker's turn ends if, in the croquet stroke, either ball is sent off court. *Exception:* for the striker's ball only, the turn does not end if a roquet is made, or a hoop or peg point is scored before going off court.

21 Continuation stroke

The striker is entitled to a continuation stroke after a hoop point is scored. A continuation stroke is also taken after a croquet stroke except when the turn ends, see law 20c, or a roquet is made on another ball.

22 Ball moving between strokes

If a ball moves between a stroke or a turn, having previously come to rest, it is replaced and the game continues. No point is scored or lost by this movement.

23 Imperfections on the surface of the court

Loose items, for example twigs or leaves, may be removed before a stroke.

Balls may be lifted out of bad holes, ruts, etc. Any such movement should not give an advantage to the striker. This may mean the movement of other balls by an equal amount to give a similar shot. In the case of a hoop attempt, it may mean moving the ball further away from the hoop.

24 Interference with a stroke

If a fixed object such as a wall or tree impedes a shot, balls may be moved subject to the same conditions as rule 23.

25 Local laws

If a lawn is to be used for an official Croquet Association event, any special conditions must be approved by the Association. For clubs or individuals, special conditions may be applied as seen fit.

Errors and interference in play

26   Definitions

Forestalling
An opponent or partner forestalls when the striker is stopped from playing due to an error or fault which has been, or is about to be, committed.

Limit of claims
This is the time after which forestalling has no effect, i.e. there is no specific remedy for the error.

Condoning
Any error or fault spotted after the limit of claims is condoned, i.e. it is allowed to stand without correction. Where there is the phrase 'Condoned if not noticed by . . .', it is followed by the limit of claims for that error or fault.

27   Playing when not entitled to do so

Examples are: playing when it is not your turn; taking croquet twice from the same ball in the same turn without running a hoop; and continuing to play having run the wrong hoop. Any such play is invalid. Balls and clips are returned to their original positions. However, such invalid play is condoned if not noticed before the first stroke of the next player's turn.

28   Playing a wrong ball

If the striker strikes either of the opponent balls, or changes to the partner ball in the middle of a turn, balls and clips are replaced in their original positions before the wrong ball was struck and the striker's turn ends. Playing a wrong ball is condoned if not noticed before the first stroke of the next player's turn.

29   Playing when a ball is misplaced – general rule

In the following situations, a ball is misplaced. If noticed, the ball(s) are replaced correctly and play continues without penalty. Misplacement is condoned if not noticed before the stroke is played.

(a)   A ball incorrectly placed after the end of the previous turn.

(b)   A ball wrongly brought back onto the yard line (see law 11).

(c)   A ball wrongly left in the yard line area or off court.

(d)   Not playing a ball from a baulk line when it should have been.

(e)   Playing a croquet stroke when the balls are not touching, or the striker's ball is touching a ball other than the croqueted ball.

(f)   Anything else not covered by law 30.

30   Playing when a ball is misplaced – exceptions

The exceptions are:

(a) Taking croquet from a wrong ball.

(b) Taking croquet from a ball which has not yet been roqueted.

(c) Not taking croquet when roquet has been made.

(d) Wrongly removing or failing to remove a ball from the game.

In all cases, the balls are replaced to their positions before the error and the striker continues without penalty, playing the correct shot. The difference between these exceptions and the general rule is that they are condoned if not noticed before the *next stroke but one* of the striker's turn.

31   Definition of a stroke and the striking period

A stroke is any movement of the mallet which is intended to strike the ball (even if it does not actually do so). Practice swings are not strokes. A stroke ends when all balls stop moving.

The striking period starts at the beginning of a stroke and ends when the striker quits his stance (this may be before or after the end of the stroke).

Note: a player may leave a ball where it is and deem a stroke to have been played.

32   Faults

The following are faults which may be made *during the striking period.* In each case, balls and clips are replaced to their original positions before the fault was committed and the striker's turn ends. They are condoned if not noticed before the next stroke but one of the striker's turn.

(a)   Touching the mallet head with the hand.

(b)   Kicking or hitting the mallet onto the ball.

(c)   Resting the mallet shaft, or a hand or arm, on the ground or the striker's legs or feet.

(d)   Not striking the ball with the end-face of the mallet.

(e)   Steering or pushing a ball, i.e. maintaining contact with it.

(f)   Striking a ball more than once, except when making a roquet or pegging out.

(g)   Touching any ball other than the striker's with the mallet.

(h)   Touching any ball with anything other than the mallet.

(i)   Crushing the striker's ball against a hoop or the peg. To be a crush, hoop, ball and mallet must be in contact at the same time (except when striking away from an obstruction).

(j)   In a croquet stroke, not moving or shaking the croqueted ball. If this fault is committed and the striker's ball also goes off court (law 20c), the opponent may choose which error and consequent remedy applies.

The following is also a fault, with the same conditions as the above, but only when a shot is hampered.

(k)   Striking the ball with the bevelled edge of the mallet face.

A shot is hampered if a hoop, ball or peg interferes with a normal shot (single ball or croquet). (It should be noted that although faults (b) to (i) can occur anywhere, they are more likely to do so in a hampered shot. Special care should therefore be taken and in the absence of an independent observer or referee, the opponent should be invited to watch the shot for faults.) *Note:* It is not a fault to strike the ball with the bevelled edge of the mallet in an unhampered shot, but this should never be done deliberately.

33   Interference with a ball between strokes

A ball that is so moved is replaced without penalty.

34   Interference with a ball during a stroke

(a)   By the striker. It is a fault under law 32 if the interference occurs during the striking period (see law 31). Otherwise the ball is replaced without penalty.

(b)   By anyone or anything else. The ball is replaced without penalty. If the ball was moving at the time, it is placed where it would have gone unless the shot was critical, for example an attempt to make a roquet, which may or may not have hit, in which case it is replayed.

35   Playing when misled

If the striker is misled because the opponent has placed the clips incorrectly, or gives false information, a replay is permitted. The replay starts from the point where the striker was first misled. The replay must not be a repeat of the original turn as the striker could not then claim to have been misled.

———————————— **Part 3** ————————————

Other forms of play: handicap play

38   Bisques

Definition
A bisque is an extra turn. It is taken directly after the end of the striker's current turn. A bisque turn must be taken using the same ball that was used in the previous turn. Bisque turns may be taken in sequence, i.e. one bisque turn can immediately follow another.

Number
The number of bisques to be given is as follows:

(a)   For standard handicap play, the higher handicap player receives bisques equal to the handicap difference of the players.

(b)   For full bisque handicap play, each player receives bisques equal to his or her handicap.

It is common to use small sticks to indicate the number of bisques left.

Faults
If a turn ends due to a fault being committed, a bisque can be used to start a new turn.

Restoration of bisques
If bisque(s) are taken in a series of consecutive turns which then turn out to be invalid and are not condoned (for example, hoops scored in the wrong order), any bisques used in error are restored.

Other forms of play: doubles play

40   General

Outline of the game
The game is played between two sides of two players. Each player has one ball and may strike only that ball.

Assistance to partner
One partner may assist the other in any way except in the actual playing of strokes or standing as a line-of-sight marker.

For doubles, the rules of singles apply, substituting 'partner's ball' for 'partner ball'. Also 'player' includes 'side' and 'striker' includes 'striker's partner'.

43   Handicap doubles play

Number of bisques to be given
(a)   For standard handicap doubles play each side adds together their handicap. The higher handicap side receives half the difference between the totals, rounded up to the nearest whole. Either player of a side may use the bisques.

(b)   For full bisque play, each player receives half their normal bisques, rounded up to the nearest whole. Players may only use their own bisques.

Faults
If a player commits a fault and the turn ends, a bisque may be taken to start a new turn but only by the player that committed the fault (except in alternate stroke doubles).

Alternate stroke doubles play
This is played in the same way as standard doubles except that each player of a partnership plays each stroke alternately. This alternation always occurs, even after faults and bisques. The second sentence of law 40 does not apply.

44   Customs of the game

Croquet relies heavily on the honesty of players. Faults and errors must be announced, even when not spotted by the opponent. Situations where faults might occur should be noted and if necessary watched by an independent observer (where available) or opponent.

The opponent should watch the game but does not have to. However, by not watching, a fault may pass the limit of claims, see law 26.

Normally, potential faults should be forestalled before they occur. Specifically however, playing a wrong ball and running a wrong hoop should only be forestalled after the fault has occurred (note that running a wrong hoop is not a fault but taking a continuation stroke afterward is).

Players should not spend too long between each shot; expedition is called for . . .

No artificial aids to play are allowed.

51 Emergency law

Situations not appearing to be covered by these laws should be dealt with as fairly as can be arranged.

9

—— FUN GAMES ——

Although croquet is a game to be enjoyed, it does require serious concentration to play it properly. The games described in this chapter are much simpler. They can be played for the odd half hour before lunch, or to relax after a concentrated game of croquet.

In all the games described, play is sequential as in golf croquet (see Chapter 3). Also, all balls which go off court or in the yard line area are replaced on the yard line.

—————————— Four-ball ——————————

A game for two or four players.

This is a similar game to golf croquet. The rules are the same as golf croquet with the following additions:

1 You gain an extra shot by either running a hoop, or hitting another ball with yours (making a roquet).

Note: The extra shot you gain by making a roquet is played from where your ball lies. You do not take croquet. Like association croquet, you can only roquet each of the other balls once before running a hoop.

2 If you hit two balls in the same shot, it is the first one hit that is roqueted. You are then allowed to hit the other one if you want to.

3 If you stick in the jaws of a hoop, you are allowed (if still there) to continue through next turn.

Robber

A game for any number of players.

1   Start anywhere on the yard line.

2   You can run any hoop in any direction. Each time that you do so, you score one point. You do not get an extra shot for running a hoop.

3   If you roquet another player's ball, you 'rob' him or her of their points. You also gain one extra shot (as in four-ball, you do not take croquet).

4   Each time you reach ten points, these are 'banked' and cannot be stolen.

For example: ROY has six points and roquets BOB who has seven points. ROY now has thirteen points and BOB has none. BOB now roquets ROY. ROY has banked ten points, so only loses three. ROY now has ten points and BOB has three.

5   The first player to reach 31 is the winner (this figure can be altered to suit the time available).

Tag

A game for three to six players.

The object of the game is to catch up with your opponents and 'tag' them, removing them from the game. The last player left is the winner.

1   Draw lots for the order of play. Alternatively, play in order of hitting ability, strongest last.

2   Players start one yard in front of their starting hoop.

3   Starting hoops are as follows:

For three players –

player one – hoop one; player two – hoop two; player three – hoop five.

For four players –

player one – hoop one; player two – hoop four; player three – hoop one-back; player four – hoop four-back.

For five players –

player one – hoop one; player two – hoop three; player three – hoop six; player four – hoop two-back; player five – hoop four-back.

For six players –

player one – hoop one; player two – hoop three; player three – hoop five; player four – hoop one-back; player five – hoop three-back; player six – penultimate hoop.

4   The route is circular and continuous. For three players the route is hoop one to six and back to hoop one again (a six-hoop loop). For four to six players the route is hoop one to rover and back to hoop one again (a twelve-hoop loop).

5   You must run hoops in a single turn. A ball stuck in a hoop can be played in either direction next turn but does not score the hoop.

6   If you run a hoop you continue your turn by one extra shot. If you run two hoops in the same stroke, you have two extra shots.

7   You may 'tag', i.e. roquet, any ball which is for the same hoop as you. Also, that ball can tag yours. Any ball which is tagged is removed from the game. Tagging gives one extra shot.

For example, at the start of a game for six players, ROY (player one) runs hoop one. The ball stops two yards from hoop two. With the continuation stroke he runs hoop two. He is now for the same hoop as player two who is in front of hoop three. He can shoot at player two. If he hits, he has tagged that player, who is removed from the game. He will also earn a further continuation shot. If he misses, he will end up close to player two who may then tag him.

He therefore does not have to shoot, but may lurk somewhere, waiting for his chance.

8   It is quite possible for players to overtake one another. A player who overtakes cannot tag the one overtaken as they are now for different hoops. The order of play remains the same.

9   If you tag a ball which is not for the same hoop, you miss the next turn and any extra shots earned for this turn.

One-ball

A game for two players.

The rules are exactly the same as for association croquet except that each player has only one ball.

Despite this rather short description, one-ball is a good game, with some interesting tactics, especially when both players are going for the same hoop. Try it and discover them for yourself!

10

—— JOINING A CLUB ——

As your game improves you will want to try your skills out against other players. The best way to do this is to join a croquet club. Here you will find a friendly atmosphere and a chance to play on full-size lawns.

If you do not know the location of your nearest club, try your local library. If they do not know, the best way to find out is to contact your national croquet association. Their addresses are given in Appendix 1.

Many clubs will have a coaching programme for beginners and improvers. You will find that having read and understood this book, you will already be well on the way to being considered an improver.

From here on, you can go as far as your ability and inclination will take you. You can simply play friendly games at your club, enjoying the company and the relaxation, or, if you want a little more competition, most clubs have a selection of events throughout the season which cater for differing abilities.

The larger clubs also run weekend and even week-long tournaments. If you want to enter these you should, if you haven't already done so, join your croquet association (see below).

Your next step upwards is to improve your play to such a standard that you will play advanced rules croquet, mentioned very briefly in this book. You can then play in advanced play tournaments, championships and, who knows, represent your country in international events.

Croquet associations

Each country where croquet is played has an organisation which acts as national representative for that country. In most cases it is called 'The Croquet Association of . . .' (followed by the country). The purpose of such an association is to act as a central body to promote and regulate croquet for that country. It will organise competitions from individual to international level. It will have membership or representation on the World Croquet Council. Affiliation to or membership of your association is very much to be encouraged because you will not only receive the benefits of membership – magazines, tournament opportunities, etc – you will be contributing to the continuance of your chosen sport.

Some associations run special events for newcomers. Where known, they are listed in the following appendix. Your association will also be able to put you in touch with your nearest club.

APPENDIX 1

Addresses of Croquet Associations

World

Secretary-General,
Mr Chris Hudson,
The Oaklands,
Englesea Brook,
Near Crewe,
Cheshire, CW2 5QW,
England.

Australia

Mrs C N Fox,
Hon Secretary,
Australian Croquet Association,
PO Box 296,
Rosney Park,
Tasmania 7018.

Nationally, events for beginners are under review. Each state also has its own association, with state-oriented tournaments.

Canada

Croquet Canada,
PO Box 892,
60 James Street,
St Catherines,
Ontario, L2R 6Z4.

England

The Secretary,
The Croquet Association,
The Hurlingham Club,
Ranelagh Gardens,
London, SW6 3PR.

England is also divided into nine regions, each with its own local federation council.

There are three national events for newcomers to croquet.

The Croquet Classic
This event is open to any player in England and Wales who has never had a handicap less than 19. It is a national event aimed specifically at garden croquet players. Preliminary rounds can sometimes be held on your own lawn. To find out details, contact the English Croquet Association.

The Golden Mallet Competition
This is a National Golf Croquet tournament open to any player who has never had a handicap less than 19. Preliminary rounds will be held locally. To find out details, contact the English Croquet Association.

National Schools Championship
This tournament is designed to encourage croquet within schools. Teams of three compete in leagues, the winners of which go forward to regional, then national, finals.

Finland

Ylöjärven Krokettiklubi,
Soppeenmäen Keskuskenttä,
Hämeenpuisto 14 A 8,
33210 Tampere.

France

Federation Française de Croquet,
4 Quai Victor Hugo,
85200 Fontenay-Le-Compte.

Guernsey

King George V playing fields.

Ireland

The Secretary,
The Croquet Association of Ireland,
c/o Carrickmines Croquet & Lawn Tennis Club,
Carrickmines,
Dublin 18.

The CAI holds a beginners tournament during the Championship of Ireland in July. Games take place under the supervision of an experienced player.

Isle of Man

Ann Cottier,
Yn Clyst,
36 Victoria Road,
Castletown, IOM.

The Manx Croquet Association holds an open singles and doubles event, the Manx Classic, in May each year.

Italy

Associazione Italiana Croquet,
Segretaria Generale,
CP 367,
21052 Busto Arsizio (VA).

A tournament for beginners is being considered.

Japan

The Croquet Association of Japan,
4-6-16,
Matsushiro,
Tsukuba,
Ibaraki, 305.

A croquet-like game called 'Gate-Ball' is also played in Japan.

Jersey

Jersey Croquet Club,
Les Quennevais Playing Fields,
St Brelade.

Kenya

H A Curtis,
PO Box 10,
Limuru.

New Zealand

The National Secretary,
The New Zealand Croquet Council, Inc,
PO Box II-259,
Wellington.

Organised coaching available to beginners.

Scotland

Hon Secretary,
13 Park Place,
Dunfermline,
Fife, KY12 7QL.

The SCA holds occasional courses for beginners.

South Africa

The Secretary,
South African Croquet Association,
PO Box 259
Constantia 7848.

Switzerland

Association Suisse de Croquet,
Peter J Payne,
En Molard-Rochau,
1261 Genolier.

Sweden

Svenska Croquetförbundet,
c/o Fred Sandström,   *or* Jan Insulander,
Elsaborgsgata 50,   Hasselstigen 38,
S-12665 Hägersten.   S-15230 Südertälje.

Courses for beginners can often be arranged on request to the association.

United States

There are a number of different versions of croquet played in the USA. Association croquet is played extensively in the west, under the auspices of the American Croquet Association.

In the east, the United States Croquet Association has its own rules. It is a sequence game with the 'yard line' being only nine inches. Although the basic strokes are the same as association croquet, this book is unsuitable for USCA rules croquet. Association rules games are, however, beginning to be played at some locations.

Anne Frost,
US Croquet Association,
500 Avenue of Champions,
Palm Beach Gardens,
Florida 33418.

United States garden croquet also tends to be played according to sequence rules, often with the old nine hoop, two peg setting.

Yet another croquet-like game is played throughout the States. This is called 'Roque'. It is played on a sandy court, ten yards by twenty, with a concrete surround, and with short-handled mallets. The headquarters are in Dallas, Texas.

In America a hoop is called a wicket and a peg is called a stake.

Wales

60 Coleridge Avenue,
Penarth,
South Glamorgan, CF6 1SQ.

The author also believes that croquet is, or has been, played in the Bahamas, Bermuda, Brazil, China, Costa Rica, Egypt, Indonesia, Jamaica, Mexico, the Netherlands, Portugal, Russia, Singapore, Spain and Tenerife.

Croquet may also be found at hotels, sports clubs and universities throughout the world – but you will probably have to ask for it!

── APPENDIX 2 ──

Addresses of Croquet Equipment Manufacturers

The Australian Croquet
Company,
1349 South Road,
Bedford Park, SA 5042
Australia

Natural Alternatives,
PO Box 2477,
Gravenhurst,
Ontario, POC 1G0
Canada

Sun Lucky Ltd,
Oimazato 3-13-6,
Higashinari-ku,
Osaka, 537
Japan

Jackson Mallets,
18 Caspar Rd,
Papatoetoe,
Auckland,
New Zealand

True-Line Croquet Equipment,
58 Wellington St,
Hamilton,
New Zealand

Barlow Balls,
Tom Barlow,
PO Box 1792,
Somerset West 7130
South Africa

John Jaques & Son Ltd,
361 Whitehorse Rd,
Thornton Heath,
Surrey, CR7 8XP
UK

Stortime Products,
Unit 14,
Southmill Trading Centre,
Southmill Road,
Bishops Stortford,
Herts, CM23 3DY
UK

Townsend Croquet Ltd,
Claire Rd,
Kirby Cross,
Frinton-on-Sea,
Essex, CO13 0LX
UK

Country Crafts,
Manor Cottage,
Widecombe in the Moor,
Devon, TQ13 7TB
UK

Woodlands Croquet Products,
Woodlands,
Skipton Rd,
Barnoldswick,
Colne, Lancs, BB8 6HH
UK

Manor House Croquet,
The Manor House,
1 Barn Croft,
Penwortham,
Preston, PR1 0SX
UK

Birkdale Croquet Equipment,
6 Walmer Road,
Birkdale,
Southport, PR8 4SX
UK

Croquet Department,
Forster Mfg Co Inc,
PO Box 657,
Wilton, ME 04294-0657
USA

Stanley Patmor,
4735 N 32PL,
Phoenix, AZ 85018
USA

—— BIBLIOGRAPHY ——

The following books are recommended by the author as good follow-on material to this book. Most are available from the English Croquet Association. The Australian, New Zealand, South African and United States associations also have their own books on sale.

The History of Croquet, by D M C Pritchard

An excellent book for those who would like to know more about the history of the game.

Plus One on Time, by D L Gaunt

A detailed look at handicap play and tactics, aimed at players in the medium to high handicap ranges.

Croquet, by J Solomon

Covers all aspects of the game up to advanced level.

Croquet, The Skills of the Game, by W Lamb

Gives a good insight into break-building techniques.

The CA Coaching Handbook

Although aimed at Croquet Association coaches, this book contains a lot of useful tips and exercises.

Laws of Croquet

The official rule book for association croquet.

Coaching Video by Joe Hogan (New Zealand)

Basic shots and techniques are demonstrated.

Croquet, Its History, Strategy, Rules and Records by J Charlton & W Thompson

This is a good beginner's guide to USCA rules croquet. It also contains sections on American garden croquet and the game of roque.

– GLOSSARY OF TERMS –

'A' baulk See **baulk**.

Advanced rules A version of croquet played at croquet tournaments which has extra rules to make the game more difficult for top level players.

Aiming point The point at which to aim in a croquet stroke when it is required that the two balls are sent in different, and predicted, directions. Also the point at which to aim in an angled hoop shot.

'B' baulk See **baulk**.

Baulk A line, one yard in from the **boundary line**, along the **yard line**, stretching from the **corner spot** at corner one to half-way along the southern yard line (**'A' baulk**) and from the corner spot at corner three to half-way along the northern yard line (**'B' baulk**). Used when starting a game and for **lift** shots.

Bisque An extra turn in a handicap game. Also the stick used to indicate the presence of such a turn or turns.

Boundary line A line, of chalk, string, etc, forming the limits of the court. The inside edge of the boundary line forms the actual boundary.

Break A turn containing more than one stroke. Sometimes referred to as an X-hoop break where X is the number of hoops scored in that turn. See also **two**, **three** and **four-ball breaks**.

Continuation stroke	An additional stroke which follows either a **croquet stroke** or **running a hoop**.
Corner	The joining points of the four **boundary lines**.
Corner area	Four one square-yard areas of the court. Their two outer edges are formed by the **boundary line**, one yard along from each **corner**. The two inner edges extend into the court and meet at the **corner spots**.
Corner spot	The innermost point of a **corner area**. A ball which goes off court one yard or less from a corner is replaced on the corner spot.
Croquet stroke	Striking your ball when it has been placed in contact with a **roqueted** ball.
Croqueted ball	The other ball (not your ball) in a croquet stroke. *Note:* before taking croquet, this ball was called the **roqueted ball**.
Crush	Forcing your ball against a hoop or the peg with your mallet. A crush is a **fault**.
Doubles	A game of croquet between four players, each playing one ball and playing as two pairs.
Double target	Two balls close to each other presenting a wide target to the striker. Three balls can form a triple target.
Drive shot	A croquet stroke played without **roll** or **stop** attributes.
Either ball rule	The rule which allows a player to choose which of the two balls is most advantageous to play. See also **sequence game**.
Error	Any action other than with the mallet which is contrary to the rules of croquet. Errors often incur a penalty. See also **fault**.
Fault	Any action with the mallet which is contrary to the rules of croquet. Most faults incur a penalty. The term foul is not used in croquet. See also **error**.

Four-ball break   A **break** using the striker's ball plus three others.

Free shot   A shot at a ball which, if missed, results in your ball going to a safe place on the court. See also **safe shot**.

Full game   A game in which the six hoops are run in both directions by both balls. A 26-point game.

Guarded leave   Finishing your turn by leaving your balls in such a way that if your opponent shoots at them and misses, you can make a **break** from the resulting situation.

Half angle   The way to calculate the **aiming point** for a **croquet stroke** which sends the two balls in different directions.

Hoop point   See **running a hoop**.

Innings   Control of the situation. A player who has such control is said to have the innings.

Jaws   The space between the uprights of a hoop.

Join up   Finishing a turn by leaving your balls close together. Careless joining up can leave a **double target**.

Lift shot   A rule by which a player may lift a ball and play it from **baulk**. A lift is given when an opponent **wires** the striker's ball.

Peel   Causing a ball other than the striker's ball to score a hoop point. If the peel occurs as a result of a **roquet** it is called a **rush peel**.

Peg out   The hitting of the peg by a ball which has scored all of its hoops. The ball is then known as a **pegged out ball**. It has completed the course and is removed from the game. The first player or side to peg out both balls is the winner.

Pegged out ball   See **peg out**.

Penultimate   The last but one hoop in a **full game**.

Pioneer   The ball sent to your next hoop but one in **three-** and **four-ball breaks**.

Pivot   The central ball in a **four-ball break**.

Push shot   A stroke in which the mallet maintains contact with the ball. This steers or pushes the ball rather than striking it. A push shot is a **fault**.

Roll shot   A **croquet stroke** in which both balls travel approximately the same distance.

Roquet   Hitting another ball with your own. A **croquet stroke** is then taken.

Roqueted ball   The ball that you have just hit. *Note:* when you play the **croquet stroke**, this ball becomes the **croqueted ball**.

Rover   A ball which has run all of its hoops. Also the name given to the final hoop of a game in a **full game**.

Running a hoop   Causing a ball to pass through its correct hoop in the correct direction. A ball which runs a hoop correctly scores a point, called a **hoop point**.

Rush   The movement of another ball which has been **roqueted**.

Rush peel   See **peel**.

Safe shot   A shot which gives little away if missed, even if your ball stops near an opponent ball.

Scatter   Striking your ball so that it hits another ball on which no **roquet** can be made.

Scoring a hoop   See **running a hoop**.

Sequence game   An old way of playing croquet in which balls were played in strict sequence. Still played in golf croquet. See also **either ball rule**.

Setting   Refers to the way that the hoops and peg are placed on a lawn. Also refers to the adjustment of a hoop to the correct width.

CROQUET

Singles	A game of croquet between two players, each playing two balls.
Stalking	The process of approaching your ball along the line of strike so that you take up the correct stance.
Stop shot	A **croquet stroke** in which the striker's ball travels only a short distance compared with the other ball.
Take-off	A **croquet stroke** in which the other ball stays virtually where it lies, while your ball is sent the required distance.
Taking croquet	The act of placing two balls so as to play a **croquet stroke**.
Three-ball break	A **break** using the striker's ball plus two others.
Tice	A ball which is placed, usually at the beginning of a game, to tempt the opponent into shooting at it and missing.
Tie	A game where the scores are equal after **time**. The game continues until one further point is scored.
Time	Both the period allowed in a game limited by the clock and the call which indicates the reaching of that limit. See also **tie**.
Two-ball break	A **break** using the striker's ball plus one other.
Wiring	A ball is wired when a player cannot strike it so as to hit any other ball. If the wiring was caused by the opponent a player may claim a **lift shot**.
Yard line	A line exactly one yard inside the **boundary line**. The line on which balls are replaced when they go out of court. The yard line is not normally marked.
Yard line area	The area between the **yard line** and the **boundary line**.

WITHDRAWN